Immediacy: The Development of a Critical Concept from Addison to Coleridge.

By

Wallace Jackson

RODOPI NV

AMSTERDAM 1973

Library of Congress Catalog Card Number: 72–93571

CONTENTS

Introduction

The academic visitor to Washington, after he passes the Supreme Court Building and the Library of Congress, comes on up to the Folger Shakespeare Library, where he sees cut in stone across the building, "THIS THEREFORE IS THE PRAISE OF SHAKESPEARE, THAT HIS DRAMA IS THE MIRROR OF LIFE." Written in 1765, this critical appraisal by Samuel Johnson no longer bespoke the highest praise for the majority of readers who purchased his edition; instead a new critical doctrine, insinuated first in the early years of the century, had by this time replaced the Italian neoclassic concept of mimesis and would, in another two decades, provide one of the touchstones for the formulation of the Romantic concept of the imagination.

Even as early as mid-century, this doctrine, which stressed the immediately affective character of art, had already pre-empted the older critical precepts and become the reigning principle of practical and theoretical criticism. Essayists as important as Burke, as insignificant as Hildebrand Jacob, and a whole gamut of commentators in-between, were writing criticism governed to a large extent by the newly evolved criterion of aesthetic affectivity. So that Johnson's splendidly ringing tribute to Shakespeare was, by the time it was written, less in the mainstream of eighteenth-century criticism than the ponderous if ecstatic remarks by John Gilbert Cooper, set forth in 1755. Taking as his text the line from *The Merchant of Venice*: "How sweet the Moonlight Sleeps upon that Bank! " he states: "That verb, taken from animal life, and transfer'd by the irresistible magic of poetry, to the before lifeless objects of the Creation, animates the whole scene, and conveys an instantaneous idea to the imagination what a solemn stillness is requir'd when the *peerless Queen* of Night is, in the full splendor of her majesty, thus lull'd to repose."[1]

1. *Letters Concerning Taste*, (London, 1755), No. vii.

Thus exemplified by Cooper, the new doctrine emphasized not the mimetic-reflective powers of the artist, but rather that special quality possessed by the highest genius for taking us directly into the ambience of his invention and causing us to experience it immediately. As such, this doctrine was developed importantly in the middle and later years of the century by critics and essayists whose attentions were engrossed by the mutually relevant subjects of "taste," "sublimity," "literary associationism," "genius," and "imagination." Consistently and steadily elaborated throughout the century, the new doctrine introduced a characteristic of response as a criterion of aesthetic value, and created a functional basis for judgment in the synthesis of man's mental faculties.

Even by the early eighteenth century it was becoming increasingly clear that the moral purposefulness of art was frequently predicated on emotive effect, that certain aesthetic characteristics occasioned an immediate response, and that this, by implication, led to serious questions about the inter-relation of moral and aesthetic values. Thus the interest in an immediate intuitive faculty, an interest sustained from Addison to Coleridge, is one of the important corollary facts of eighteenth-century literary theory. "We are struck," says Addison in Spectator 411, "we know not how, with the Symmetry of any thing we see, and immediately assent to the Beauty of an Object, without enquiring into the particular Causes and Occasions of it."[2] Some hundred years later the modulated echo of this comment reaches us from the pages of Coleridge's essay "On the Principles of Genial Criticism": "*The sense of beauty subsists in simultaneous intuition of the relation of parts, each to each, and of all to a whole: exciting an immediate and absolute complacency, without intervenence, therefore, of any*

2. *The Spectator*, ed. Donald Bond, (Oxford: Clarendon Press, 1965), III,538.

interest, sensual or intellectual."[3] It is, thus, with the
continuous effort made throughout the century to locate in
man's mind an intuitional principle to explain both his aesthetic
judgments and his capacity for aesthetic creativity, that this
study is concerned. Hopefully, the work will contribute to the
history of literary criticism a record of that unifying principle
which brought together the various orientations of eighteenth-
century criticism within a broad pattern of relevance.

This work is, it seems to me, in the pattern of scholarship
that has grown out of Samuel Holt Monk's classic treatment of
The Sublime.[4] Following his lead, recent studies have
emphasized the progressive and accretive nature of literary
debate in the eighteenth century. The old shibboleths have been
laid to rest. It is no longer feasible to think in terms of
arbitrarily closed compartments of literary thought, no more
than it is wise to demarcate boundaries or areas within the
archaic terms of pre- or post-romantic. Traditions blur and fuse;
ideas inter-penetrate and cross-fertilize. One task of the scholar
is to point out how ideas, like Lucretian atoms, link together to
form new and surprising shapes, disintegrate and come together
again in still more surprising and unexpected configurations.
Yet all is not mere anarchy. The eighteenth century was
forming its own image of man, shaping a criticism to fit that
image, and perhaps under the impress of some unconscious

3. *Biographia Literaria,* with his *Aesthetical Essays,* ed. with introd. by
J. Shawcross (London, 1958), II, 239.

4. *The Sublime: A Study of Critical Theories in XVIII-Century
England* (New York, 1935). Professor Monk states as his purpose the
"detailed study of one of the leading aesthetic ideas in eighteenth-century
England. Beauty, sublimity, taste, imagination, and the picturesque are the
most important of these ideas. Their rise, transformation, and progress are
interesting and the complete history of any one of them should throw
light upon the progress of taste, the change of values, and the gradual
growth of critical and aesthetic theories in the period that lies between the
flourishing of neo-classicism and the triumph of romanticism . . ." (p. 2).

wisdom preparing a legacy of ideas that would go into the making of later thought.

Such speculations will not, I hope, be taken as the symptoms of bemusement, the self-indulgent reveries of a midnight pondering student. The problem was what the problem always is: what is man? New tools for this inquiry were forged in the seventeenth century and tested in the eighteenth. If we begin with Locke, Professor Tuveson has instructed us that we will end in the aesthetics of romanticism.[5] It is precisely this approach that I wish enthusiastically to emulate. In the spirit of Walter Bate's shifting premises of taste,[6] or Gordon McKenzie's study of the psychological

5. E.L. Tuveson, *The Imagination as a Means of Grace: Locke and the Aesthetics of Romanticism* (Berkeley and Los Angeles, 1960). Tuveson's thesis begins with an exploration of the new Lockean epistemology and the implications that arose from it, and directed the course of speculative literary thought. The shifting of the principle of reality to the subjective human consciousness prepared for a theory of the imagination as "both a means of receiving . . . the impressions of a nature that is an unfoldment of divinity, and, also, a creator of illusion shows after the manner of divine art" (p. 115). The romantic concept of the imagination has its roots in Locke's "sense of the living activity of the mind in all its phases . . ." (p. 41).

6. W.J. Bate, *From Classic to Romantic: Premises of Taste in Eighteenth-Century England* (Cambridge, Mass., 1946). Bate derives the principle of "romantic relativism" from Shaftesbury and his followers. He argues that British empiricism forms the groundwork for "the somewhat heterogeneous body of assumptions . . . which is called romanticism" (p. 94). Addison's aesthetic categories are linked by Bate to the romantic stress on "suggestiveness" in art as an end in itself. He adds that as empirical psychology was fast culminating in a complete skepticism of immutable reason and ideal nature, "the extorting of a subjective activity in comparing and combining ideas became not merely a conscious aim but one of the fundamental purposes for the very existence of art" (p. 100). He explores the relation of British associationism to subjectivism and emphasizes the increasing elasticity of the meaning of imagination in later eighteenth-century thought.

current,[7] I have turned to my own inquiries. I have, it will be
seen, taken such hints quite literally and emphasized the organic
continuity of eighteenth-century criticism. I have tried to trace
a theme that runs now in shallow, now in deeper beds of
thought, that like Coleridge's sacred river now disappears
entirely only to break forth more vehemently. That this is so is,
I hope, not more poetry than truth, not more fancy than fact.
So that in writing this book my first task was to study the
fascinating history of a theme in criticism; my second to reveal
the urgencies that compelled this theme on its progress; my
third to show the figure that thought makes.

The work is composed of four chapters, each of which
corresponds to a different historical period and phase in the
development of my theme. The first chapter discusses the
beginnings of affective literary theory in Addison, Shaftesbury,
and the Abbé du Bos, and comprises the period from the late
Restoration to the death of Addison in 1719. Here I treat of the
genesis of immediacy as a criterion of ontological value to
Addison and to Shaftesbury, and as a standard of purely
emotive effect to the Abbé du Bos. The second chapter reviews
the critical situation during the years 1719-1744 as it is
pertinent to comparative evaluations of the sister arts, poetry
and painting. The relation between immediacy and pictorial

7. Gordon McKenzie, *Critical Responsiveness: A Study of the
Psychological Current in Later Eighteenth-Century Criticism (Berkeley and
Los Angeles, 1949)*. McKenzie states that "The importance of the
psychological approach as one of the great transitional links in the history
of thinking about books can hardly be overstated. This type of thought
completes the account in the history of criticism of the gradual shift from
an examination on a neoclassical basis of the external work of art to an
attempt to understand and evaluate literary experience on the basis of the
reactions of talented readers. It embodies the transition in method, in idea,
and in motive, from Pope's *Essay on Criticism* to Coleridge's *Biographia
Literaria.* It is in itself one important strand of criticism which develops
continuously throughout the century . . ." (p. 5).

values, and the transitional characteristics of pre-mid-century criticism constitute the major topics of this inquiry. The third chapter isolates three specific transitional topics at mid-century: the shift from a mimetic to a pragmatic bias; the decline of pictorialism in eighteenth-century criticism; the problem of immediacy in terms of its relevance to taste and associational criticism. As a criterion of aesthetic value, immediacy is further studied in relation to the works of Hogarth, Burke, Webb, and Kames. The fourth chapter details the history of immediacy in expressively oriented theories, particularly those concerned with the concepts of genius and imagination in the later eighteenth and early nineteenth centuries.

It has not been my purpose to quarrel with the interpretations of other scholars. I have presented my own views on those subjects that have been commonly discussed and have acknowledged my frequent indebtedness to those scholars whose arguments I have employed to strengthen my own. Naturally, areas of disagreement exist. I concur for example, with W. J. Hipple's statement that "It is a curiously perverse tendency among modern scholars to argue that the philosophical critics of the eighteenth century, by tracing aesthetic responses to their roots in passions, senses, faculties, and association, subvert the neo-classical system of rules and absolutes, and thus open the way to rampant subjectivism."[8] The tendency to rampant subjectivism was seldom if ever a problem in eighteenth-century criticism, but if a determined attempt was made to maintain the neoclassical absolutes, it was certainly not, as the century developed, on the basis of a neoclassical system of rules. This indeed is part of the exciting complexity of thought that the age experienced. The neoclassical system of rules (and can we agree on a single moment of consensus and codification?) was structured on the foundation

8. W.J. Hipple, Jr., *The Beautiful, the Sublime, & the Picturesque in Eighteenth-Century British Aesthetic Theory* (Carbondale, 1957), p. 119.

of seventeenth-century rationalism, and survived intact and unimpaired only so long as that remained whole and entire. By 1700 classical rationalism was in the throes of a death agony, its confident assumptions of right reason as a ruling principle of mind already under serious attack. Surely no dedicated effort was made to "subvert" the neoclassical system, but the implications of sensationalism and empiricism opened the way for inquiries into the nature of man that were not in harmony with that neoclassical image of him.

Nor can I pass over René Wellek's neglect in confidently attributing many pre-Coleridgean ideas to German sources alone. To speak, for example, of "Kant's analysis of taste" as "an intermediate faculty between intellect and the senses"[9] is almost willfully to disregard the formation of this concept in Addison and others. Nor does it seem appropriate to suggest that "the Kantian way" for deciding "the universality of taste" is that "we involuntarily claim that all other minds ought to think and feel the same,"[10] without indicating that Kames had been quite as obstinate much earlier. Nor again is it judicious to remark that Kant had considered the sublime as subjective ("No object of sense is sublime in itself, but only as far as I make it a symbol of some Idea."[11] without noticing the independent development of this concept in the British tradition by Archibald Alison. Finally, though Wellek states that "As in Schelling or the Schlegels the poet is both conscious and unconscious,"[12] this idea is given some credence by Shaftesbury, and his influence would have helped keep it alive during the century.

On occasion I have found that my own estimations of

9. René Wellek, *A History of Modern Criticism: 1750-1950,* Vol. II: *The Romantic Age* (New Haven, 1955), 161.

10. *Ibid.*

11. *Ibid.,* 160

12. *Ibid.,* 163.

minor eighteenth-century essayists are somewhat higher, or lower, than those accorded them by others. Infrequently I have entered some small plea for some now forgotten critic, if not entirely on the basis of his intrinsic distinction, then because of the light he sheds on the historical situation. Daniel Webb is one such case. I cannot quite concur with Professor Monk's judgment that he "wrote much, but said little, on the arts of painting, poetry, and music."[13] I have sometimes found it necessary, however, to spend time on essayists who are beyond redemption. For this I ask the reader's patience in the hope that some pretension to a breadth of inquiry will justify the risk of occasional tedium.

Yet I do not assert definitiveness. Some writers whose commentary bears lightly upon this study have been excluded. When it has seemed to me that the remarks of an essayist did not materially enhance or forward my arguments, as in the case of Dennis's inquiry into the sublime,[14] or add significantly to earlier critical positions, as is so with Hutcheson, I have restricted my treatment of him to an infrequent reference. I do not believe that the main lines of inquiry have suffered by these omissions. My method has been regulated by my intention, and my whole effort has been to bring to light a theme which was instrumental in forming and shaping much of eighteenth-century theory and criticism.

13. Monk, p. 108.
14. On this subject see Marjorie Hope Nicolson, *Mountain Gloom and Mountain Glory: The Development of the Aesthetics of the Infinite.* (Ithaca, 1959), pp. 276 -289.

Chapter One

Immediacy: The Argument from Design

By 1700 the tripartite structure of neoclassical aesthetics was beginning to show signs of radical strain. The basic and interlinked doctrines of nature, reason, and mimesis had entered the last period of their vitality, and the slow, painful process of feeling along the ways of change had begun. Early eighteenth-century aesthetics shared of course the suppositions of seventeenth-century rationalism, were leagued with it, and drew validity from it. That art is the mirror of nature, as nature is the image of God, was an argument from analogy, and from this depended the seventeenth-century concept of mimesis. Basically, this concept was predicated upon the operative laws of uniformity and regularity, upon the notions of fixity and stasis beyond the human condition. In the fullness of time, empiricism was to vitiate entirely the bases of rationalism and to challenge the frail evidence for a universe operative according to the principles of uniformity and regularity.

Sensationalist psychology was shortly to derogate reason to the status of meddler. In the new epistemology, Professor Tuveson has suggested, "the stronger the sense impression, the deeper it penetrates into the depths of the mind and the more likely it is to evoke a meaning that lies outside the scope of the understanding."[1] Implicit is the suggestion that the strength of a sense impression is proportionate to the degree it escapes classification by the reason. Where mimesis, in the hands of Restoration practitioners, had found sanction in the promulgation of its chief purpose, the rational grasp of the ideal, and where this ideal had found its complement in a sustained skepticism of passion or enthusiasm, the Lockean epistemology

1. Tuveson, pp. 76 -77.

opened the way for a theory that ideas within the mind associate involuntarily. Furthermore, the fact of involuntary association did not merely reintroduce the Restoration bogey of lawless subjectivism and the anarchy of private impulse. It did, however, tend to shift the basis for moral purposefulness from nature to human nature, and suggested that the inherent structure of the human mind provided, if only that structure were known, a sufficient and adequate guide for moral conduct. The task that now loomed ahead was one of sustained empirical observation of the human sensory and intellectual equipment, a task that ultimately led to the riot of faculty psychology much later in the century. But in the early 1700's the promise was still fresh. To follow nature was clearly intended as an injunction to follow human nature.

This new freedom, this Lockean emancipation of the subrational characteristics of the mind, coincided fortuitously with the decline of seventeenth-century rationalism. As Cassirer notes, "Spinoza's equation of God and nature," postulating the "uniformity of nature . . . [on] the essential form of God," rested on a now decadent metaphysical assumption.[2] This once bright concept, the principal axiom of rationalism, had dwindled into mere habitual faith. It became increasingly clear that the axiom of uniformity in nature was predicated solely on an assumption derived from experience. We are all familiar with what use Hume made of this reflection, but it is important to remember, and even by an act of historical imagination to comprehend, the role and place of uniformity in Enlightenment thought. Cassirer has made this especially clear: "The uniformity in nature springs from the essential form of God; from the very concept of God it is clear that He can be thought of only as One, as in harmony with himself, as unchangeable in all his thoughts and acts of will. To suppose a change of

2. Ernst Cassirer, *The Philosophy of Enlightenment* (Princeton, 1951), p. 57.

existence as possible in God, would be tantamount to a negation of his essence."[3]

If there is no sanction for an inference that proceeds from God to nature, there is no more justification in the inference that proceeds from nature to God. The metaphysics of Spinoza were trapped within the circle of his own logic. A convenient way, it appeared, for avoiding this logical snare was to shift the premises for uniformity from metaphysics to the biological and sociological nature of man. Just this was attempted by the academician s'Gravesande in his inaugural address before the University of Leyden in 1717. s'Gravesande argued, in effect, that it is the nature of man to require and expect uniformity, that his expectations unsatisfied would destroy empirical existence and vitiate man's purposefulness. Further, what is in the nature of man to require must have been implanted in him by the author of his being. That reasoning which proceeds from nature to God is thus proper and necessary, for the "author of nature has made it necessary for us to reason by analogy, which consequently can be a legitimate basis for our reasoning."[4] This cleverly conceived argument is flawed, however, by the habit of analogy which exercised so potent an influence over Enlightenment thought. s'Gravesande has unwittingly returned to the exact metaphysical sanction for uniformity in God and nature that his argument was designed to avoid.

The case is typical. s'Gravesande is betrayed by the *a priori* assumption and elevates a seeming empirical certainty into a metaphysical certainty. Most importantly, the customary metaphysical route from nature to God now seemed closed, and a chasm between God and nature threatened to open. It is just at this period in Western thought that aesthetic speculation achieved an urgency it had not hitherto possessed. It began to

---

3. *Ibid.*
4. s'Gravesande, *Physices Elementa,* as quoted by Cassirer, p. 61.

be clear to some few minds that aesthetics offered a viable route to God, and it is, I think, no mere historical accident that critical attention began to turn to the characteristics of the art object and the precise nature of its ontological effectiveness. In the light of these considerations, the period witnessed the publication of two important documents, the Earl of Shaftesbury's *Characteristicks* and Addison's *Pleasures of the Imagination.* It is to the second of these, which began to appear in serial publication on Saturday morning, June 21, 1712, that I want first to be attentive.[5]

In the first several papers, Addison's attention is directed principally to four important topics: the perfection of the sight above the other senses; the division of the pleasures of the imagination under two heads; the three sources of all pleasures of the imagination: the great, the uncommon, and the beautiful; the relation between nature and art and the pleasure they provide the imagination. These topics form the foundation of Addison's aesthetics, and only after he has set them forth does he then, in *Spectator* 415, offer to "throw together some Reflections on that Particular Art, which has a more immediate Tendency, than any other, to produce those primary Pleasures of the Imagination, which have hitherto been the subject of this discourse."[6] Addison, we remember, had defined the primary pleasures as those which "entirely proceed from such Objects as are before our Eyes," whereas seondary pleasures "flow from the Ideas of visible Objects, when the Objects are not actually before the Eye, but are called up into our Memories. . . ."[7] This, to one of Addison's readers, would be sound and familiar theory, its patent derived from Hobbes and the distinctions sustained by Locke. Addison repeats the formula and then turns to his real

5. *The Spectator,* ed. Donald Bond, (Oxford: Clarendon Press, 1965).

6. *Spectator,* III,553 — hereafter the vol. no. will be omitted since all subsequent citations are from the same volume.

7. *S.* 411, 537.

subject in *S.* 415: "*Greatness,* [which], in the Works of Architecture . . . [relates] to the Bulk and Body of the Structure, or to the *manner* in which it is built."[8]

For the moment, however, let us return to Addison's earlier discussion of greatness in order to have the whole of his thought on this subject before us as we proceed. By greatness, he has said, he does "not only mean the Bulk of any single Object, but the Largeness of a whole View, considered as one entire Piece."[9] He has given as examples those unbounded prospects in nature which fling the mind into "a pleasing Astonishment."[10] For, the "Mind of Man naturally hates every thing that looks like a Restraint upon it. . . ."[11] From this he has adduced the principle that such "wide and undetermined Prospects are as pleasing to the Fancy, as the Speculations of Eternity or Infinitude are to the Understanding."[12] The conjunction is of course provocative and provides a hint, in the manner of Addison's typically understated style, of what lies ahead. In *S.* 415 he carries this discussion a step further and inquires into greatness of manner: "Among all the Figures in Architecture there are none that have a greater Air than the Concave and the Convex. . . ."[13] This observation finds empirical verification in all the practice of ancient and modern architecture. The reason must be, he continues, "because in these Figures we generally see more of the Body, than in those of other Kinds." In bodies other than the concave and convex, "the Sight must split upon several Angles, it does not take in one uniform Idea . . . Look upon the Outside of a Dome, your Eye half surrounds it; look up into the Inside, and at one Glance you have all the Prospect of it; the entire Concavity falls into your Eye at

8. *S.* 415, 553.
9. *S.* 412, 540.
10. *Ibid.*
11. *Ibid.*
12. *Ibid.* 541.
13. *S.* 415, 557.

once. . . ."[14] One uniform idea: "We are struck . . . with the Symmetry of any thing we see, and immediately assent to the Beauty of an Object, without enquiring into the particular Causes and Occasions of it."[15]

Thus and so far, greatness of manner is conjoined with one uniform idea. The occasion of pleasure rests upon an empirically derived principle; namely, that the mind is inherently disposed to respond uniquely to uniformity, and historical precedent is called upon for sanction and confirmation. Furthermore, the pleasure that uniformity evokes is immediate; it does not require the sanction of judgment or the inquiry of the reason. We see, and in the fulness of our seeing, we immediately assent. Uniformity as an aesthetic value is verified by the immediacy with which it communicates pleasure to the perceiving mind.

It should be apparent that Addison's reflections have little to do with the usual generic considerations that normally form the staple of neoclassic inquiry. He pays no attention here to a theory of kinds nor, for that matter, to nice distinctions of emotive effect. He is interested only in an unspecified "pleasure" or "pleasures." We cannot attribute a necessary cause to this pleasure, "because we know neither the Nature of an Idea, nor the Substance of a Human Soul. . . ."[16] Consequently, "all that we can do, in Speculations of this kind, is to reflect on those Operations of the Soul that are most agreeable, and to range under their proper Heads, what is most pleasing or displeasing to the Mind. . . ."[17] If, however, we can produce no necessary cause for our pleasure, we may yet be able to offer a final cause:

One of the Final Causes of our Delight in any thing that is

14. *Ibid.*
15. *S.* 411, 538.
16. *S.* 413, 545.
17. *Ibid.*

great, may be this. The Supreme Author of our Being has so formed the Soul of Man, that nothing but himself can be its last, adequate, and proper Happiness. Because, therefore, a great Part of our Happiness must arise from the Contemplation of his Being, that he might give our Souls a just Relish of such a Contemplation, he has made them naturally delight in the Apprehension of what is Great or Unlimited.[18]

This argument neatly parallels s'Gravesande's in kind; it begins with a psychological assumption and proceeds to a metaphysical one. It, too, proceeds from the implicit analogical proposition that argues from man to God, from a supposed urgency of being to the location of that cause in the mind of God.[19]

The great and the uniform impress the mind naturally; that is, they impress *all* minds and all minds immediately. Distinctions of reason and judgment are invalidated, and degrees of understanding are beside the point, since no conclusions by the reason or by the judgment are called for. The immediacy of our assent is a proof of the universality of the principle. The immediate pleasure in the great and uniform merely confirms a fundamental and inexorable *law* of being. The passage from man to God is kept open and secure by the pleasures of the

18. *Ibid.*

19. See Miss Nicolson's discussion of Addison and "the psychological basis of man's feeling for the 'great' " in terms of the natural sublime (p. 315). She does not develop the position that for Addison art, as well as nature, served the same purpose of leading man's thoughts back to God. She writes: "Addison was urging upon his contemporaries the necessity of man's looking directly upon Nature and realizing that the stimulus that came from painting or poetry was 'secondary' " (p. 310). My own treatment of Addison is intended to develop the view that the stimulus from art was, indeed, "primary," because in art (particularly architecture) the "great" and the "uniform" came together in the harmony of synthesis. See my discussion below.

primary imagination. That this is Addison's intention is further confirmed by two circumstances over which it might be well to pause. The first of these is that Addison, his purpose accomplished, dismisses any further consideration of the way architecture utilizes the new and the beautiful to convey pleasures. The second requires a little further attention to one of Addison's more curious propositions. This is, if "the Products of Nature rise in Value according as they more or less resemble those of Art, we may be sure that artificial Works receive a greater Advantage from their Resemblance of such as are natural. . . ."[20] This neat distinction points to the necessity for an approximate mean condition between the irregularities of nature and those too regular productions of art which restrict the imagination to a "narrow compass."

On the other hand, the wilder and more irregular scenes of nature stimulate the associative imagination and promise a degree of pleasure perhaps otherwise unattainable. Furthermore, a variety of radical stimuli may act to awaken, and bring to the surface of the mind, ideas that now slumber in the memory. Thus the cognitive value of irregular images is not entirely to be overlooked. On the other hand, Addison's critical pre-dispositions have been formed essentially by the principle of Restoration aesthetics. It is precisely here that the confrontation of diverse values takes place in his thought; here it is that the new and the old, the principles of empirical psychology and the emphasis upon order and decorum come together in Addison's criticism. The synthesis he proposes is to take from nature the grand and the august and to fuse with them the perfect pattern and design of art. It is on the basis of this alliance, as it is developed in *Spectator* 414, that Addison makes the transition from the "great" (*S.* 413) to the "uniform" (*S.* 415).

By the early eighteenth century art had become the channel leading to the contemplation of God; numerous rele-

20. *S.* 414, 550.

vant problems were subsequently to arise, and they will provide us with plentiful material for reflection in the following chapters. But the pertinent problem posed for Addison was to find an empirical basis for the moral consciousness. In order to do so, it was necessary to avoid the assumptions predicated on the *a priori* reason, assumptions which had vitiated seventeenth-century rationalism. What Addison realized, most importantly for the future of British aesthetics, was that the work of art, characterized by order, uniformity, and design, activated the imagination to the perception of an analogous order immanent in the universe. The mind was led upward to God through the perception of forms organized in space and time. Experience, not reason, was summoned to verify this proposition and experience indicated that the proposition was true. Furthermore, the experience itself was characterized by an immediate pleasure, an instantaneously received delight, which ruled out any mediating act of reason or judgment. That this may have led to an undue optimism, an unsustainable confidence in the nature of man and in the beneficence of God's plenitude is clearly arguable. But the optimism, at the very least, was not naive; it was born out of the urgency of a collapsed metaphysical system. Therefore, Addison says, in a tone that may easily seem too triumphant to us, "We are struck . . . with the Symmetry of any thing we see, and immediately assent to the Beauty of an Object, without enquiring into the particular Causes and Occasions of it." And to this Shaftesbury echoes, "What is it but *the Design* which strikes? "[21]

For Addison, as we have seen, the mind of man was moved to the contemplation of God through the aesthetic medium of the great and the uniform. In Shaftesbury, the experience of divine universal order is attained through the phehomenon of the beautiful. Like Addison, Shaftesbury cir-

21. "The Moralists; A Philosophical Rhapsody," *Characteristicks,* II (1732), 405.

cumvents the office of the understanding as an instrument of the moral consciousness and proposes a new and distinct faculty which acts involuntarily to awaken man to the perception of divine order. Addison's primary imagination is necessarily postulated upon a theory of the mind's essential endowment; the nature of which is that certain kinds of objective phenomena necessarily evoke certain kinds of emotive effects because it is in the nature of mind so to respond.[22] This hypothesis is confirmed by the immediacy of our response which Addison uses as an ontological principle of being. To much the same purpose does Shaftesbury develop his theory of a reflex or internal sense.[23]

In attacking what he assumed to be the inevitable drift to moral relativism consequent upon Locke's epistemology, Shaftesbury developed two primary positions. The first is that an internal sensation, an "Idea or Sense of *Order* and *Proportion*," is imprinted on our minds and interwoven with our souls.[24] This impression directs us, at some unspecified stage in

22. Cf. Edward A. and Lillian D. Bloom, "Addison's 'Enquiry after Truth': The Moral Assumptions of his Proof for Divine Existence," *PMLA*, LXV (1950), 198-220. See this useful article for a corollary discussion of Addison's "proof" in terms of prevalent concepts derived from natural science, psychology, and metaphysics.

23. See C. DeWitt Thorpe, "Addison and Hutcheson on the Imagination," *ELH*, II (1935), 215-234. Thorpe points out that "where Shaftesbury assumed that God had implanted in man's mind certain materials for its use: natural ideas of virtue and goodness, natural images of perfect form, of harmony and symmetry and proportion; Addison felt that God had so made man's mind that it would act so and so in response to such and such physical stimuli. There is a wide difference between these views" (224). He adds that "before Shaftesbury, Descartes, Hobbes and Locke had all noted, in direct statement or by implication, the existence of a sort of sixth sense which has to do with internal impressions of pleasure or pain" (229).

24. "The Moralists," *Characteristicks*, II, 284.

our maturity, to perceive immediately the difference between uniformity and irregularity. This indwelling power is the common possession of all men, but is specifically evoked by the harmonious proportions of the beautiful which leads the mind from the microcosmic to the macrocosmic order. Through the phenomenon of the beautiful, the mind awakens to "the mutual Dependency of Things! "[25] and witnesses the successive exfoliation of systems opening beyond systems. His second position has to do with the peculiarly sympathetic powers that he attributes to genius. Genius is characterized by being in special proximity to nature. A plain, internal sensation may perceive harmony and order, but the special gift of intuitive immediacy, the distinction of genius, penetrates beyond form to the forming power. Matter is merely the guise of mind; the real achievement of the artist-genius is to make this truth experientially viable by assuming in his own character the role of "second Maker."[26] The artist's function is, on a lower scale, a re-enactment of original, formative power.

Physico-theological theory was in extreme danger of becoming remote, a collocation of mechanistic metaphors without any real congruity to human experience. In celebrating enthusiasm, Shaftesbury threw the whole weight of his argument against the center of deistical doctrine and developed a vitalistic principle to serve as a counterpoise to mechanism. Enthusiasm, however, is carefully delimited as the special prerogative of genius, its tenure restricted to those moments of inter-communication between artist and nature.[27] The empha-

25. *Ibid.*, 287.

26. "Advice to an Author," *Characteristicks,* I, 207.

27. On this subject see W.J. Bate, "The Sympathetic Imagination in Eighteenth-Century English Criticism," *ELH,* XII (1945), 144-164. Bate notes that "A belief in the importance of the poet's 'enthusiastic' absorption in his subject, with the resulting obliteration of his own identity, appeared early in eighteenth-century criticism. Shaftesbury,

sis, naturally if not intentionally, worked against the principle of decorum and against the idea of art as technic or craft. On the other hand, however, this was not a dangerous concession, since the final product, the work of art itself, could be checked against the principles of uniformity and design. In this way, excesses of zeal or frenzy could be constrained, and practical criticism was left with a guide to remonstrate against merely private fancy.

The peculiar ambiguity of Shaftesbury's position is that if he moves away from the center of neoclassic theory, he insists still upon accord with the usual characteristics of neoclassic art. His major importance is that he sought a principle of unity within the psyche and located this principle in an internal faculty which participated equally in man's emotive and rational nature. In the mind of genius this essentially passive faculty is transmuted into an essentially active faculty, since genius is endowed with the capacity for intuitional immediacy. It is for this reason that the nature of genius is more important to Shaftesbury than to any of his British predecessors, and it is due to his treatment of this topic that Shaftesbury can move aesthetics into the center of metaphysics. Now it is the artist who through the "Power in Numbers, Harmony, Proportion and Beauty of every kind . . . naturally captivates the Heart, and raises the Imagination to an Opinion or Conceit of something *majestick* and *divine.*"[28]

It is the artist who, through his construction of the beautiful, holds the key to the Platonic harmonies of the true, the beautiful, and the good. Since by definition their co-existence is assured, the experience of the one guarantees the experience of the others. None of the falsities to which the

indeed, who was always prone to emphasize the necessity of 'enthusiasm,' almost anticipates the language of Keats's famous contention that the true poet 'has no character . . . no identity' " (149).

28. "Miscellaneous Reflections," *Characteristicks*, III, 30.

understanding is liable can intrude, since the experience of the beautiful is characterized by the same immediate apprehension which Addison, following a different route, also offered as verification.

In using the aesthetic experience as the route to moral consciousness, neither Addison nor Shaftesbury developed any very clear epistemology. Among the many problems they bequeathed to their followers was the precise relation between the immediate effect communicated by certain kinds of phenomena and the epistemological structure of the mind. Was the nature of the mind such as to provide an infallible instrument on which immediate effects could be registered to raise the mind to moral perceptions? If so, what were the exact components of this instrument, and to what extent did it incorporate the traditionally higher and lower faculties of the mind? If genius is recognizably different in degree or organization of common powers, how is that difference to be explained? These and many related problems form the staple of eighteenth-century inquiry. In their basic form, they provide much of the material for subsequent critical and aesthetic theory. Primarily, however, Addison and Shaftesbury constructed the bridge between the aesthetic and the moral on the basis of the immediate effect, which had only to be felt to be acknowledged. Their emphasis represents the incipient signs of change in critical orientation discussed above.

Mimetic theory did not of course wither overnight. Both Addison and Shaftesbury imbued it with some new vigor, and it is clear that their intentional bias was to provide a new premise for this valued remnant of the classical past. If mimesis could no longer be sustained by the postulates of rationalism, then, hopefully, it could find sanction in an ontological principle, some necessary and inherent disposition of the mind. In effect, however, their achievement was pragmatic; that is, they drew attention from the work of art to the audience, and located in the immediate effect one of the paramount conditions of the aesthetic experience.

Inevitably this was so; their work fell in with the momentum of empiricism, which was irresistible by 1700, when Locke appended his chapter "Of the Association of Ideas" to the fourth edition of *Human Understanding.* Neither Addison nor Shaftesbury was particularly fortunate in his direct successors;[29] the implications of their ideas remained undeveloped until almost mid-century, and then they tended to merge into the main stream of the Longinian sublime and to be distorted in the long tortuous debate over faculty psychology. To a large extent, Locke's sensationalist psychology helped to obscure and overbalance the aesthetico-moral speculations of Addison and Shaftesbury. Professor Tuveson has pointed out that "The solution to the [epistemological problem] . . . was to endow the mind, not with completed ideas, but with the power to make all its ideas out of impressions."[30] This shift of the locus of reality to the human mind, with a corollary emphasis upon subjective processes, prepared the way for aesthetic criteria that would evaluate the work of art totally in terms of its effect upon the mind. It subsequently allowed for an emotionalistic aesthetic, certainly perverting Locke's intention, but nevertheless building upon implications he had offered.

In the hands of little-gifted critics, the rich emotive possibilities of art were cut off from the high moral theme it had been the labor of Addison and Shaftesbury to construct. Essentially, the theme of immediacy declined to become associated with immediate gratification of the senses, and emerged as a maxim of practical criticism. The authority for

29.   Thorpe wishes to establish the "fact that Hutcheson's emphasis on Addison's theories and his approval of them must have had much to do with directing attention to them and spreading their influence among later writers and thinkers" (233 -234). I agree, but if Hutcheson participated in the wider dissemination of Addison's ideas, he, by Thorpe's own admission did not much advance them.

30.   Tuveson, p. 16.

this application was of course latent. Writing in the late seventeenth century, Dryden had remarked that "the advantage of painting, even above Tragedy, [is] that what this last represents in the space of so many hours, the former shews us in one moment. The action, the passion, and the manners of so many persons are to be discerned at once, in the twinkling of an eye. . . ."[31] And Shaftesbury had suggested that "the fewer the Objects are [in a painting], beside those which are absolutely necessary in a Piece, the easier it is for the Eye, by one simple Act and in one View, to comprehend the *Sum* or *Whole*."[32] But neither Dryden nor Shaftesbury was proposing mere emotive affectivity as a distinctive criterion of value. Yet it was just this attribute of painting — that it communicates immediately — that was to become most important to the aggregation of petty essayists who followed upon the death of Addison in the third and fourth decades of the century.

Certainly the complementary relationship between the arts, the theme of *ut pictura poesis,* whose respectable pedigree reaches back to Horace and Simonides, and the conventional bases for the sisterhood of the arts, were familiar and acceptable.[33] By the early seventeenth century, poetry and painting had something of an equivalent standing. Their similarity was seen to reside in "a like nature, and both . . . busie about imitation"; their complementary relation secure in that both arts "invent, faine, and devise many things, and accommodate all they invent to the use and service of nature."[34] Yet, to a

31. "A Parallel of Poetry and Painting," *Essays of John Dryden,* ed. W.P. Ker, 2 vols. (New York, 1961), II, 131.

32. "A Notion of the Historical Draught or Tablature of the Judgment of Hercules," *Characteristicks,* III, 383.

33. William K. Wimsatt, Jr. and Cleanth Brooks, *Literary Criticism: A Short History* (New York, 1959), pp. 263-264.

34. Ben Jonson, "Timber, or Discoveries," in *Critical Essays of the Seventeenth Century,* ed. J.E. Spingarn (Oxford, 1957), I, 29.

certain extent, the mediaeval prejudice favoring the intellectuality of the verbal arts persisted, and any final verdict declaring for the superiority of the one art to the other would admit that "of the two the Pen is more noble then the Pencill: For that can speake to the Understanding, the other but to the Sense."[35] Robert Wolseley, writing in 1685, reiterates Jonson's classical formula: "Poetry is *Pictura loquens* and Painting is *Poema silens*; that paints with Words and this speaks by Colours."[36] Wolseley adds that no two things in the world have a closer affinity, for "to make a very like Picture of any thing that really exists is the perfection as well of Poetry as Painting."[37]

Such judgments rested upon the classical theory of mimesis and upon the principal assumption inherent in mimetic theory: that art was a microcosmic reflection of the larger, macrocosmic order. Renaissance and Restoration theorists in general, however, tended to pervert the strictly classical interpretation of mimesis, and insisted usually upon a more literal interpretation, restricting the artist to the imitation of external forms and the *natura naturata*. For this reason, among others, by the late seventeenth century much of the resilience and much of the latitude for the free play of the artist's experience within a normative doctrine had gone out of mimetic theory. As a doctrine of aesthetics, mimesis had both hardened and narrowed, its principal emphases restrictive rather than permissive. When in the latter years of the seventeenth century a change in critical orientation began to appear, the change reflected a shift in bias from the art object, governed by fixed and immutable laws, to the subjective processes of the mind by which art is experienced and inwardly assimilated.

This shift posed several serious problems. A pragmatic bias, which looks from the work of art to the audience and

35. Spingarn, I, 29.
36. Robert Wolseley, "Preface to Valentinian," in Spingarn, III, 17.
37. *Ibid.*, 22.

locates in the immediate effect one of the conditions of the aesthetic experience, is liable to be attractive to different, and indeed opposite, value systems. It can raise the unholy spectre of subjectivism. Addison and Shaftesbury had proposed that the complex sensibility of the mind is under the arbitration of an inherent, indwelling principle of lawfulness; that the immediate emotive experience is not wanton and capricious, but is a profoundly rich occasion for moral knowledge. In man's sensible and emotive nature they found a principle for the integrity of being. On the other hand, the way was open for the immediate emotive effect to be considered an aesthetic value without moral implications or overtones. It was of course possible to argue from the vantage of the sensationalist epistemology that the stronger the sense impression, the more immediate and intense, the more likely it was to evoke an associational pattern of potential cognitive value. Yet it was clearly possible to ignore the cognitive value of sensations and arrive at a pleasure principle based on immediate and intense stimulations.

It is this principle that is taken up in 1719, the year of Addison's death, by the French critic, the Abbé du Bos. Du Bos is that model of knowing connoisseur and witty arbiter, thoroughly familiar with recent developments in English philosophy and literature. He had met and come to know Locke during a visit to London, at which time he compared the French translation of *Human Understanding* with the original English. His *Reflections* show the influence of the Lockean epistemology, which he used as a sub-structure for his own emotionalist-oriented theories of art. In its main concerns, du Bos's position is both bold and limited. He allows an unusual licence to sensibility as the mediator of judgment and holds that the pleasurable feelings evoked by the work of art are the final warrant of aesthetic merit. His idea of mimesis resides in the wholly debilitated notion that the principal merit of poems and pictures consists in the imitations of such subjects as would have excited real passions. Other than this, he makes no real distinction between the impressions received from art and those from nature.

Like all critics and aestheticians of the period, he holds the bias which favors sight as the principal sense, but unlike most he employs the bias to argue the comparative superiority of painting to poetry. Words can affect us only by degrees; they excite ideas which the mind must afterward turn into pictures if we are to be moved and engaged.[38] Appropriately, this critical principle is developed in terms of the machine, the metaphor for the Lockean epistemology: "All these operations, 'tis true, are soon done; but it is an incontestable principle in mechanics, that the multiplicity of springs always debilitates the movement, by reason that one spring never communicates to another all the motion it has received."[39] Deduction consequently affirms that immediacy of representation is the superior instrument of pleasure. In painting, we "behold . . . at one immediate view, things which in verse are represented successively only to our imagination."[40] From this he moves ingenuously to the position that tragedy may be more affecting than any single painting, but only because the "poet presents us successively with fifty different pictures, as it were, which lead us gradually to that excessive emotion, which commands our tears. Forty scenes therefore of a tragedy ought naturally to move us more, than one single scene drawn in a picture."[41]

It is perfectly consistent with this point of view that du Bos has little to say about form or design, and because his strictures so narrowly contain the aesthetic experience (he does not recognize it as more than pleasure), he necessarily over-

38. *Critical Reflections on Poetry, Painting, and Music* (London, 1748). I, 323.
39. *Ibid.*
40. *Ibid.*
41. *Ibid.*, 329.

emphasizes the values of novelty and surprise. His evaluations of impressions tend thus to become quantitative rather than qualitative. Novelty and surprise have no necessary relation to form or design, and what distinguishes the true poet from the indifferent versifier is that the latter may "by dint of consultation and labor form a regular plan . . . but 'tis he only who is blessed with the genius of the art, that is capable of supporting his verses with continual fictions, and with fresh images rising at every period."[42]

Du Bos entirely circumvents the role of reason in aesthetic judgment and banishes it entirely except as it may "account for the decision of our senses. . . . The decision of the question does not belong to the jurisdiction of reason. . . ."[43] The impulse toward complete subjectivity is checked somewhat by a "sixth sense [which] we have within us. . . . This is, in fine, what is commonly called sense or sensitive perception."[44] This unaccountable sense (the *je-ne-sais-quoi* of the mind) is not exactly what in the English tradition is known as "taste." British essayists never so entirely removed taste from a close relevance to reason, or never so entirely surrendered to man's sensible nature. Du Bos went much further and in doing so established himself as supporting the radical extreme of emotionalist theory. He was well known to subsequent British critics, although he failed to develop any real followers among them. His principal importance for us today is that he suggested one possible employment for the criterion of immediate effect. He explored an avenue of possibility and almost exhausted it; at the very least he made that exploration unnecessary again for the English critics of the eighteenth century.

Fortuitously, his theories accorded well with the new empirical psychology and had the seeming sanction of being

42. *Ibid.*, 236.
43. *Ibid.*, II, 238.
44. *Ibid.*, 239.

epistemologically sound. His emphasis coincided with the general neoclassical demand for simplicity in all the arts. Lovejoy has suggested that simplicity was "in part a manifestation of a general dislike for intricacy and complexity. A complex design does not reveal itself to the eye at once; it imposes upon the beholder, hearer, or reader a special effort of comprehension, an effort difficult for all, and probably impossible for some; and it is sufficiently condemned by that fact alone."[45]

The criterion of immediate affectivity, its moral and ethical significations, coincided exactly with the dominant motifs of Enlightenment thought. And here as usual, critical formulations were predicated on the prevalent and dominant cosmology. Intricacy and complexity were at odds with the simplicity of the world machine and with the growth of natural religion in the Restoration and early eighteenth century. On the authority of Locke, the works of nature "everywhere sufficiently evidence a Deity." It is but opening the eye and letting the truth enter, for through "natural revelation . . . the Father of Light, and fountain of all knowledge, communicates to mankind that portion of truth which he has laid within the reach of their natural faculties."[46] The emphasis, then, was upon that body of "common notions" which so well accorded with eighteenth-century conceptions of plenitude and the harmonies of the *consensus gentium.*

The principle of immediacy seemed to fit very well into this scheme, promising an avenue to man's entire nature and so to that greater Nature toward which he yearned in the nostalgia for ancient harmonies. But beyond the potential ontological significance which the principle of immediate emotive effect

45. A.O. Lovejoy, "The Parallel of Deism and Classicism," *Essays in the History of Ideas* (Baltimore, 1948), pp. 95 -96.

46. *An Essay Concerning Human Understanding,* ed. A.C. Fraser, 2 vols. (New York, 1959), II, 431.

suggested, it was soon seen that immediacy had bearing as a maxim of practical criticism, and opened up new possibilities for comparative estimations of the sister arts. Du Bos suggested as much. Furthermore, immediacy accorded well with pictorial values, and with the notion that the aesthetic object was essentially something to be visually realized.

It was commonly assumed, as du Bos's reflections on words would indicate, that the sense of sight, above all sensory apparatus, was in immediate proximity to the imagination, and that consequently what directly appealed to the vision would, all other necessary conditions being satisfied, more likely produce the pleasures of the imagination. Under the impress of sensationalist psychology a host of petty critics examined the relative merits of poetry and painting in terms of immediate affectivity. Already at hand was the authoritative formula, *ut pictura poesis*; the new standard of immediacy acted to revitalize it, and in the conjunction of the two the Augustan essayist found a basis in principle to satisfy a critical temper that was, or thought of itself as, well-rooted in the classical past. It may very well be the case that the importance now given to immediacy and totality of perception, as primary aesthetic criteria, is distinctly related to Locke's insistence upon clear, intuitive knowledge as the first of our certainties. The etymology of *intuition,* from the Latin *intuere,* would, in any event, harbor provocative implications and almost certainly be a factor contributing to the early eighteenth-century bias for pictorial values. These values, their development in the hands of critics of the third and fourth decades, and the relation of pictorialism to immediacy, provide matter for the next chapter.

Chapter Two

Immediacy: The Rivalry of Sisterhood

In 1695 when Dryden's attention was called to the
complementary relation between the sister arts, he added, as we
have seen, one distinctive note to an otherwise complacent
comparison. Working well within the usual pattern, his essay
pairs the epic poem with the history painting, comedy with
genre painting, and farce with the pictorially grotesque. These
parallels are casually conventional, unsustained by any hint of
serious inquiry. As typical pairings they are repeated by Dennis
in 1702,[1] and form the familiar staple of comparative assumptions in early eighteenth-century discussions of the sisterhood.
John Hughes, in 1715, somewhat expands the theme by stating
that the resemblance of the one art to the other is more
particular in allegory, since this more nearly is "a kind of
Picture in Poetry."[2] These comments indicate the general range
of English criticism on the subject at the time. The usually
unexceptional verdict: "the Pen is more noble then the Pencill,"
dictated the terms of the inquiry while severely limiting its
extent.

It is only after the major critical adventures of the second
decade that these terms begin to show signs of inadequacy and
become relatively inconsequential. They endured and served
their purpose so long as the assumptions on which they rested
were secure. These assumptions were born of the habit of
analogy, and sustained in the metaphors of mirror and reflection. They were the product of a critical system which placed
the locus of reality outside and apart from the human being,

1. "Large Account of the Taste in Poetry," in W.H. Durham, *Critical
Essays of the Eighteenth Century, 1700-1725* (London, 1915), *passim.*
2. "On Allegorical Poetry," in Durham, p. 88.

and they were further dependent upon the conventional hierarchy of faculties derived from Renaissance tradition.

But the early years of the century suggest the incipience of a uniquely modern condition which has its basis in the Cartesian dualism. By a laborious act of self-scrutiny the mind was encouraged to regard itself, to witness its own native and inherent tendencies, and to be present, as it were at its own making. Given this as one of the conditions of the empirical spirit, the mind of Western man has never been quite integral, whole, or at ease with itself since. Withdrawing into itself, it has ultimately come to ask everything of itself. This indeed is a long story and a small part only of the historical self-consciousness of the early eighteenth century. Yet it is a part of this history, for the theme of immediate emotional affectivity became a criterion of aesthetic value when the modes of criticism turned from the art object to the mind regarding that object.

My purpose in this chapter is to look briefly at the situation in comparative criticism of the sister arts during the years 1719-1744. By the early eighteenth century, affective theory had seriously disordered the neo-classical establishment, and its claims were challenging the tenure of older values. Pictorialism, among the latter, tended toward the static representation of figures in a landscape, and so did not seem to fit into a criticism increasingly oriented toward the values of literary psychologism. The result was that painting, in the years directly preceding mid-century, was depressed well below poetry, and the higher, more broadly humanistic function of the latter was not again seriously rivaled by its sister art.[3] Theater, and especially tragedy, became the ideal medium because it presented through picture and language the kind of inquiry into human nature in which the age was interested.[4]

3. Wimsatt and Brooks, p. 266.
4. See L.A. Elioseff, *The Cultural Milieu of Addison's Literary Criticism* (Austin, 1963), pp. 74-94, for a discussion of the relation between theater and morality in neoclassic criticism.

Yet in the rivalry of sisterhood, painting held the advantage of superior affectivity; it could communicate immediately, through natural signs, without translation, and was happily free of cumbersome ambiguities that retarded the reader's easy access to specific meaning. These were the criteria that the advocates of a more broadly humanistic aesthetic encountered; in the end they carried the day, but the older arguments persisted. One solution was to import the criterion of immediate effect into a system of values that supported poetry over painting. This was both obvious and inevitable strategy, since immediacy was intrinsic to affective theory and few essayists ignored its claims. No one of these writers left a significant impress upon the criticism of the period; in the aggregate only can they help us to understand the historical moment which followed upon the work of Addison and Shaftesbury.

In Jonathan Richardson's "Essay on the Art of Criticism" (1719), we can witness the formation and gathering of assumptions derived from the previous work in epistemology and literary theory, and the transmutation of these into critical premises. Where Dryden in 1695 could define invention as "the disposition of the work; to put all things in a beautiful order and harmony, that the whole may be of a piece,"[5] Richardson's "Essay" suggests that the definition is already outmoded and inadequate. The point is of course that the new epistemology quickly and effectively took hold and became part of the standard equipment offered by any claimant to critical notice. On this basis Richardson rejects Dryden's regulative "invention," suggesting that impressions stored in the memory are "sometimes compounded, and jumbled into forms which nature never produced. . . ."[6] We create necessarily after the pattern of images stored in the mind, but the volitional control exercised over them is at best loose and haphazard. Reason, as a

5. Ker, II, 139.
6. *Works* (London, 1792), p. 157.

regulative agency, is assigned something very proximate to a negative function. Intrusive upon the imaginative activity of the artist, it can reduce or hinder the progress of his composition, but has little to do with bringing it to perfection.

This loosening of rational strictures prepares the way for new aesthetic emphases. Thus, drawings may be in some ways superior to paintings, as the latter may reflect the loss of original creative impulses and so seem only a "sort of copying from those first thoughts...."[7] Consequently, Richardson is ready to approve highly irregular form as evidence of the artist's immediate response to nature, and a necessary condition of that response. Though he offers a system of rules for the art of criticism, he requires also that judgment be based on "the intrinsic qualities of the thing itself...."[8] His position is not entirely atypical, and the difficulties that arise stem from his own inexact notion of the relation between externally derived criteria and those suggested by the work of art itself, between rules and the *sui generis* quality of each particular work. He is most frequently informative despite himself, and in him we can read the contradictions of criteria that are and remain in restless incompatibility.

The problem basically was that Richardson attempted to append criteria to the older Restoration critical structure without fundamentally disturbing it, and he finally is unwilling to realize the implications of his own tentative formulations. He is best and most consistent in treating of pictorial values as he does effectively in his earlier essay, "The Theory of Painting." His position here is based on two premises: that painting is the better vehicle for the transmission of ideas because it "pours" them into the mind, filling the mind immediately, whereas words only "drop" ideas and lift "up the curtain by little and little."[9] Richardson's bias implicitly favors

7. *Ibid.*, p. 121.
8. *Ibid.*, p. 111.
9. *Ibid.*, p. 6.

the immediate emotive effect, which is best satisfied by the visual arts. Like du Bos, he makes the emotive response and the imaginative stimulus dependent upon the primary sense of sight, a point of view hardly unusual at this period.

Secondly, as ambiguity inevitably attends upon the word a loss of clarity and distinction is unavoidable: "Words paint to the imagination, but every man forms the thing to himself in his own way; language is very imperfect..."[10] There are an infinite number of referents for which we have no exact denotations, but the painter so conveys ideas — through the medium of natural signs — as to be universally understood.

Theater differs from both poetry and painting as it is "a sort of moving, speaking pictures," and so has somewhat the best of both, "but these [pictures] are transient; whereas painting remains, and is always at hand."[11] Most importantly, the stage never represents things truly, especially if the scene is remote and the story ancient. Clearly Richardson's inquiries have led him to the poles of contemporary opinion. He emphasizes unambiguous clarity and historical veracity, but does not detect the contradiction between these criteria and his liberating defense of irregularity and spontaneity, or "first thoughts" as he terms them. These widely varied critical sympathies, an amalgam of old and new criteria, serve to suggest the deep impress left upon the critical tradition by Hobbes's aesthetic dicta.

First, by divorcing wit from fancy, then by making subordinate the former's original imaginative signification, and finally by depressing almost entirely the element of fancy, Hobbes introduced into British criticism a definition of wit as an essentially judicious and discrete act of mind. The problem facing Richardson was that of restoring the imaginative licence to composition while maintaining, *contra* Hobbes, the basic

10. *Ibid.,* p. 6.
11. *Ibid.,*

truthfulness of art. For this reason, Richardson is at some pains to defend irregularity, not as symptomatic of disordered fancy, but as an indication of the fresh and unmediated response to nature. For this reason also, he attempts an incomplete and unfortunately unconvincing defense of the essential heterogeneity of each work of art. So too does he understate the role and function of reason in composition. What disappoints is that Richardson, on the threshold of the key problems of imaginative licence and original genius, turns away to the prosaic counters of conventional opinion.

The occasional glimmering attempts to wed neoclassic precepts to subjective licence turned, however, on the increasingly decisive criterion of immediacy. Even such excessively cautious essayists as Hildebrand Jacob are clearly aware of immediacy as a value and, in the pattern of Addison, suggest that art should cause us to "conceive all at once" that order which is like nature itself.[12] Jacob echoed Richardson's commentary on the occasional superiority of drawings to paintings, joining Richardson's delight in irregularity to that pleasure afforded observers who "may find Matter enough to exercise their own *Imaginations upon* ... *by those Sketches* ... which are but lightly *touch'd,* [and] seem sometimes to have more *Spirit,* and often *please* more than such as are perfected."[13]

It would be a matter of serious misapprehension to assume that such views were unrelated to the morally instrumental function of art. Indeed, these newly emergent criteria are designedly open routes to moral purposiveness. Such pathways are among those leading eventually to the full development of the sublime, in which to the stimulus of irregularity are added the phenomena of the great and overpowering. It

12. "Of the Sister Arts: an Essay," *The Works of Hildebrand Jacob* (London, 1735), p. 398.
13. *Ibid.,* p. 405.

should, however, be perfectly clear that subjectivism posed no real threat to the critical establishment in these still early years; it was, at least in its moral intentions, deeply rooted in traditional convictions. Pictorialism emphasized clear and distinct ideas and thus served these convictions. Repeatedly, the essayist whose attention is engaged by comparative evaluations dwells on the picture-forming capacity of the sister arts.

Behind this bias is of course the hugely authoritative figure of John Locke. Locke had set the sanction of his judgment on imagistic criteria: the poetic image delights the mind which, "without looking any further, rests satisfied with the agreeableness of the picture and the gaiety of the fancy."[14] As late as 1740, George Turnbull is content to echo this sentiment, noting that "there is indeed no other way of trying the Propriety, Force and Beauty of a poetical Image, but by considering the Picture it forms in the Imagination, as a Picture."[15]

Pictorialism represented something like the surety of comprehension; an image in the mind was not an ambivalent, elusively ambiguous quality, like a word, radiating diffuse meanings. Instead it was fixed and static. Pictorialism shut out what could not be reduced to the clear and distinct, along with all of that which did not proclaim its immediate and definite relevance to the mind perceiving.

On the basis that poetry and painting are to be compared as pictures, Turnbull lays out his criteria. These consist of rather familiar precepts, occasionally derived from Shaftesbury, though showing also the signs of Richardson and other precursors. Turnbull's principal emphasis falls upon "easiness or unity of sight," requiring that in "a poetic Whole, the same regard ought to be had to the Memory, as in a Painting to the Eye."[16]

14. *An Essay Concerning Human Understanding*, I, 204.
15. *A Treatise on Ancient Painting* (London, 1740), p. ix.
16. *Ibid.*, p. 80.

To such points as these he is meticulously attendant and writes presumably with the Aristotelian maxim of a "certain magnitude" in mind: a painting should be neither too large to be comprehended in a single view nor too small to satisfy the requisite union of greatness with uniformity. Theater, however, and the citation is conventional, best satisfies easiness of comprehension by observing the prescriptive unities of time, place, and action.

The point of view maintained throughout the *Treatise* results finally in a *reductio* which places poetry as a subspecies of painting. Though Turnbull rehearses the unity of all the arts and officiously lards his arguments with classical authorities, though he is careful to assert the equal range and capacity of both arts, their value as instruments of pleasure and instruction, clearly "Poetry is only able to accomplish these Ends as it is a Painting Art; or since what renders it so excellent in moving and instructing us, is its being able to rear up, by Words, in the Imagination, true consistent lively Pictures."[17] As a uniquely verbal and non-visual art, the only advantage poetry attains over painting is the provision of "proper Language to each Character and Personage. . . ."[18]

Turnbull was a follower of Shaftesbury; this is evident not only in the general tone of the *Treatise,* but in the remarks on the mind and the relation between creativity and the moral sense: "There is implanted in our Minds not only a strong desire of understanding Nature's Methods of Operation, and all its various Appearances; but also a very strong Disposition to imitate Nature, emulate it, and vie with it; and thus to become as it were Creators ourselves."[19] To this disposition Turnbull attributes the origin of all the "noble and aspiring, imitative Arts." Those "very same Faculties and Dispositions which

17. *Ibid.,* p. 182.
18. *Ibid.,* p. 148.
19. *Ibid.,* p. 136.

qualify us for understanding and relishing the Beauty and
Perfection of Nature, the Beauty and Perfection of moral
Conduct, and the Beauty and Perfection of the imitative Arts is
so evident, that it is indeed unaccountable how any who
pretend to Taste or Intelligence in these Arts, can doubt of the
Reality and Naturalness of Virtue, and of a moral Sense in our
Make and Frame. . . ."[20]
    In this one long pronouncement, Turnbull asserts the
correspondence of nature, moral conduct, and the imitative
arts, and subsequently proceeds to the conclusion that "the
Perfection of the imitative Arts consist[s] . . . in making regular
and beautiful Systems, in which every part being duly adapted
and submitted to what is principal, the Whole hath a great,
noble, and virtuous Effect upon the Mind . . ."[21] This is somewhat watered-down Shaftesbury, with nothing of Shaftesbury's
mystique of the alignment between man and nature, and the
shared sense of formative power in man and nature. Turnbull's
"moral sense" is a merely compartmental faculty isolated from
the enormous complexity of sensational impressions and passional impulses. What is dangerous in Shaftesbury, those hints at
vague and unexplored recesses within the mind and the willing
commitment to rapture, Turnbull had no taste for whatever.
    The *Treatise* is a useful example of what had happened to
Shaftesbury by near mid-century; even by 1740 there was no
clearly demarcated way beyond him, and to go beyond was to
crack, once and for all, the harmony of normative experience
and universal moral order. On the threshold of this adventure,
the essayists of the third and fourth decades hesitated. What
compelled them beyond was a condition to which they had
already become attached, without perhaps realizing its eventual
significations. As early as Addison and Shaftesbury, the integrity of reason and emotion had been breached, and the focal

20. *Ibid.*, p. 137.
21. *Ibid.*

point of moral knowledge had been located in the immediate emotive effect of art. The implications of this fact were not always understood by their followers, but the distinction was usually preserved. Turnbull, for example, maintains that pleasure is consequent upon immediate effect, but separates this from the rational inquiry into the causes of pleasure. To a large extent, this of course is merely following Locke, but Locke gave no indication that the pleasurable feelings that attend the aesthetic experience could lead to anything beyond. Pleasure was pleasure indeed, but almost everything that had serious implications for the human condition was dissociated from aesthetic delight.

In the pull of opposite tendencies a compromise frequently resulted. The essential nature of this compromise was to grant that beauty is perceived immediately, without the employment of the reason, but that the reason is later used to understand the characteristics of beauty. In this compromise, reason and emotion have no integrated function, but remain as strangers to each other, one coming in as the other goes out.

> The Perception of Pleasure called Beauty . . . is distinct from the Reflexion upon Utility, or upon Regularity and Unity, it [beauty] is perceived immediately, or at first sight previously to all Considerations of these Concommitants. These Connexions between Beauty, Regularity and Utility, are found out afterwards by Enquiry. . . .[22]

This situation was to plague British criticism through the century; it is one of the conditions leading to faculty psycholo-

22. *Ibid.*, p. 139. This distinction is essentially Addisonian. Hutcheson, as R.L. Brett comments, also distinguished between two kinds of beauty: one is "immediately apprehended," the other "is seen only after reflexion and consideration of the subject." "The Aesthetic Sense and Taste in the Literary Criticism of the Early Eighteenth Century," *RES*, XX (1944), 199 -213.

gy and that entire prolonged attempt to reintegrate reason and emotion. It should also be noted that emotion is discussed without the attribution of specific qualities; that is, little if any attention is given to the diversity and variety of emotive reactions at this point in time. There seems little general feeling for the nuances of pleasure or pain, or any attempt to correlate these with specific forms of art. This would of course suggest that for most essayists of the period, the specific quality of the emotion was not important because the essayist's eye was, so to speak, on the purpose served and not on the precise characteristics of the feelings evoked. It may be that there was no vocabulary at hand for this inquiry, but had there been a need for this sort of study, a vocabulary would have developed to satisfy it. The fact is that subjectivism, as we understand the term, had made no serious incursions into critical attitudes. If it had, criticism would have broadened into studies of the more generally purposive functions of art.

This did not happen in the years before mid-century because pictorialism depressed serious inquiry into the inter-relations of the human sensory apparatus, and so acted to narrow or restrict consideration of the affective range of art. Moreover, pictorialism helped forward a criticism which stressed visual immediacy and valued the aesthetic object in proportion to its capacity to evoke an immediate emotive effect. Immediacy, prescriptively applied, contributed to the reduction of the size of the aesthetic unit: in tragedy to the single scene, in descriptive poetry to the image. The traditional superiority of poetry to painting had rested upon the former's "more noble" appeal to the understanding, but the criterion of immediate emotive effect cut across traditional values and served also to truncate the formal characteristics of art.

Such tendencies in criticism were necessarily unfavorable to the verbal arts since the criteria they fostered could not possibly come to terms with genres that depend upon cumulative effects, significant shifts in tone, and inevitable variations of pace. When the redress of critical imbalance developed, it drew strength from the growing emphasis on the sympathetic relation between art and observer. As a principle of the eighteenth-century critical apparatus, "sympathy" is most usually and markedly associated with Adam Smith's *Theory of Moral Sentiments* (1759), and the literary psychologists' use of it as an ethical concept.[23] As a critical principle, "sympathy" suggested a means of effective insight into character and situation and served as a regulative guide for moral behavior.

As early as 1729, James Arbuckle (whose name should stand as a synonym for obscurity) had suggested that that kind of poetry is best which gives "the truest and liveliest Representation of what passes in the human Mind on any incident or Occurrence in Life."[24] Descriptive poetry, though agreeable "to a well-form'd Imagination," does not raise those "wonderful Emotions" which attend the recital of actions accompanied by dangers, and with "the various Sentiments which arose in the Mind on such Occasions."[25] The nameless principle on which

23. Meyer H. Abrams, *The Mirror and the Lamp* (New York, 1953), p. 245. See also W.J. Bate, "The Sympathetic Imagination in Eighteenth-Century English Criticism," *ELH*, XII (1945), 144-165. Bate suggests that "the development of the sympathetic imagination as an aesthetic doctrine came largely from a group of Scottish critics who tended to agree with Archibald Alison's estimate of the *Moral Sentiments* as 'the most eloquent work on the subject of Morals that Modern Europe has produced,' and who felt with James Beattie that 'the philosophy of Sympathy ought to form a part of the science of Criticism' " (148-149).

24. *A Collection of Letters and Essays*... lately published in the *Dublin Journal* (London, 1729), I, No. 50, Saturday, March 12, 1725/6. Cf. Bate, "The Sympathetic Imagination in Eighteenth-Century English Criticism": "James Arbuckle ... writing soon after Shaftesbury, had explicitly stated the indispensability of the imagination, which he considered divinely implanted, for sympathetic knowledge of others" (148).

25. Arbuckle, *loc. cit.*

Arbuckle's reflection depends clearly anticipates Burke's popular dictum that the business of poetry and rhetoric is "to display rather the effect of things on the mind of the speaker, or of others, than to present a clear idea of the things themselves."[26]

In the years preceding mid-century, the most important attempt to draw upon this principle is Charles Lamotte's *Essay upon Poetry and Painting* (1742). Lamotte shows some fair amount of familiarity with criticism of the sister arts, has obviously read attentively the earlier works by du Bos and Richardson (both of whom he mentions by name), and writes as an antagonist of pictorial values in literature. Against the pictorialism of du Bos and Richardson, he urges the greater range of psychological exploration available to the verbal arts, and his work does stand as a portent of later critical studies. His arguments are frequently both ingenuous and shrewd, and occasionally display those odd turns of thought suggestive of a mind working well apart from the usual patterns of Augustan criticism. To the familiar touchstones of pleasure and instruction, he brings a blend of simple parochial bias and debating skill. "Pictures," he solemnly warns us, "are the Books of the Ignorant" and often worshipped as images. Yet he admits the justice of Richardson's observation that painting "pours Ideas into the Mind, but Words only drop them," and acquieses in the opinion of du Bos that painting does its business faster, disclosing the whole scene in the glance of an eye and displaying all its beauties and excellences at once, whereas the progress of poetry is more gradual.[27]

However, as the verbal arts are more suited to convey and express mutability, so conversely the visual arts, limited in time and space, "must render the Pleasure by Degrees faint and

26. *A Philosophical Enquiry into the Origins of our Ideas of the Sublime and Beautiful*, ed. J.T. Boulton (New York, 1958), pt. v, sect. 4.
27. *An Essay upon Poetry and Painting* (Dublin, 1742), p. 29.

languid, and at last tire and surfeit the Beholder."[28] Where a painting can show only one passion in a single figure at one time, a poem can draw aside the curtain on all the different "Motions and Passions of the Soul," and exploring all those hidden features of the personality, engage more profoundly with the whole man than the resources of painting allow.[29] Against the usually telling argument of immediate effect, Lamotte offers the neglected empirical observation that people are seen to weep at a tragedy, but experience has indicated no one in tears before a painting.[30] He cites du Bos to the effect that tragedy contains an infinity of pictures and so must necessarily be more affecting, and counters with the suggestion that were a painter to draw many different scenes leading the viewer to the pathos and catastrophe of the story, the effect would not equal that of one single scene in a tragedy.[31]

At the center of Lamotte's *Essay* is the conviction that poetry is a superior means for moving the passions because it is a superior instrument for probing them. To this end he is quick to seize the limitations implicit in pictorial immediacy and to imply that poetry probes the hidden figurations of the soul which, in their complexity and variety, are not equally representable by a merely visual medium. In formulating his criteria, Lamotte seems less interested in the socially regulative function of art than in art as a medium for psychological inquiry. The notion that art serves as a ladder to God is no real part of his critical appartus. His *Essay* is one of the earliest eighteenth-century attacks upon pictorial values, although his position *vis à vis* immediacy is strained and ambiguous. He seems to wish to dissociate pictorialism from immediacy and argues, at one point, that poetry, communicating through the

28. *Ibid.*, p. 25.
29. *Ibid.*, p. 26.
30. *Ibid.*, p. 30.
31. *Ibid.*, p. 31.

various senses, can reveal "in an instant" all the characteristics of personality.

Essentially, Lamotte had set out to reassess the traditional relationship of the sisterhood. That this task should have attracted some urgency is apparent in the emergence of new criteria which compelled a revaluation. The subject was not unpopular, and in 1744 James Harris, with a more comprehensive and methodical plan, re-examined the field. Like the others who precede him, Harris cuts no notable figure today, and his reputation depends from the somewhat fragile thread of his *Three Treatises*. It is to the second of these, "A Discourse on Music, Painting, and Poetry," that we will be attentive. At the beginning Harris states the premise that will guide his study:

> In entering upon this Inquiry, it is first to be observed, that the MIND is made conscious of the *natural World* and its Affections, and of other *Minds* and their Affections, by the several *Organs of the Senses*. By the *same Organs* these Arts exhibit to the Mind *Imitations,* and imitate either Parts or Affections of this *natural World,* or else the Passions, Energies, and other Affections of *Minds.* There is this Difference however between these *Arts* and *Nature*; that Nature passes to the Percipient thro' *all* the Senses; whereas these Arts use only *two* of them, that of Seeing and that of Hearing. And hence it is that the *sensible Objects* or *Media,* thro' which they imitate, can be *such only,* as these two Senses are framed capable of perceiving; and these Media are *Motion, Sound, Colour,* and *Figure.*[32]

He proposes to judge the merit of the arts by two criteria: mimetic accuracy and the kind of subject imitated: fidelity and value. His method establishes a basis for comparison

32. *Three Treatises* (London, 1772), pp. 55 -56.

by detailing a fairly comprehensive catalogue of subjects peculiarly suited to each art. Painting he limits to all things and incidents characterized by figure and color, music to those of motion and sound. Poetry, however, imitates through all the "media" and includes in itself all that can be accomplished by the visual or auditory arts.[33] His discussion gains something in range and depth as he compares music with poetry, poetry with painting, and painting with music in terms of the special "media" used by each. For example, on the basis of imitation through sound and motion, the merits of poetry and music appear equal; music seems better to imitate motion in nature (greater variety), whereas poetry is more accurate in the imitation of natural sounds (greater verisimilitude).[34]

These comparisons, to which sundry qualifications are attached, tend to become rather elaborate and more than a little confusing. This sort of scheme is usually, and here as well, accompanied by an unconscious distribution of unequal emphases, and does not much more than chart the bias of the author. But this itself is a point of interest, and his handling of the relation between poetry and painting requires our attention. Painting best imitates those subjects *"whose Comprehension depends not on a Succession of Events: or at least, if on a Succession, on a short and self-evident one – which admits a large Variety of such Circumstances, as all concur in the same individual Point of Time, and relate all to one principal Action."*[35] The direct allocation of immediate affectivity, as the distinctive characteristic of painting, along with its greater capacity for mimetic fidelity, necessitates the rule that "IN

33. *Ibid.,* p. 70.
34. *Ibid.,* pp. 73-74.
35. *Ibid.,* p. 77. See Jean Hagstrum, *The Sister Arts: The Tradition of Literary Pictorialism and English Poetry from Dryden to Gray* (Chicago, 1958). Hagstrum notes: "The 'picturesque' in neoclassic poetry may be elucidated if we inquire what the critic and aesthetician understood to be

ALL SUBJECTS, WHERE PAINTING CAN FULLY ASSERT ITSELF, THE IMITATIONS OF PAINTING ARE SUPERIOR TO THOSE OF POETRY...."[36]

Harris's thesis turns on two distinct and opposed meanings of nature. Painting is a faithful image of spatial phenomena; employing natural signs it appeals "thro' the Medium of Nature," whereas poetry must communicate through an artificial "Medium of Compact" [language].[37] On the other hand, poetry is a representation of human nature, its subjects "so framed, as to lay open the *internal Constitution of Man,* and give us an Insight into *Characters, Manners, Passions,* and *Sentiments*";[38] subjects that are the "most *affecting*; the most *improving*; and such of which the Mind has the *strongest Comprehension,"* and to which we are "of all the *most intimately related."*[39] The essential meaning of nature is split decisively: nature is both the mind and all that pertains to it, and the nonself or all that is external to being. *N*ature vs. *n*ature.

This distinction was of course implicit in the premises of his "Discourse" quoted above. But the distinction has become something more that that in the course of argument; it has become a conflict. Weighing Nature against nature, Harris declares for the latter; language is the only medium imitative of psychological and emotive phenomena in a clear, precise, and definite way, "as they in Nature stand allotted to the various sorts of Men, and are found to constitute the several Characters

the most important characteristic of painting. It was simply this: painting was able to produce its effect all at once in a single pregnant moment. A truly imitative art, its physical details coexisted simultaneously, like those of nature" (p. 159).

36. *Ibid.,* p. 79.
37. *Ibid.,* p. 77.
38. *Ibid.,* p. 84.
39. *Ibid.,* p. 85.

of each."[40] An accurate conception of character can be gathered only from a *"Succession of various and yet consistent* Actions; a Succession enabling us to *conjecture,* what the Person of the Drama will do in the *future,* from what already he has done in the *past.* "[41]

Here is a pressure point in eighteenth-century aesthetics and criticism. Addison and Shaftesbury had held consistently a view of man under the aegis of eternity, and employed the principle of immediate emotive effect as a guarantee of man's innate orientation to God. In splitting nature into two essential meanings, Harris helped forward the notion that man is explicable as a socio-psychological being; that is, his nature can be studied apart from the ontological problem. Harris's position was not uncommon; it was part of the tendency toward critical psychologism, which regarded the work of art as a behavioristic tool. As this impulse strengthened, pictorial values declined, and comparatists less and less reckoned the relative superiority of the sister arts. Painting was considered an art of imitation, whereas the more broadly purposive function of poetry resided in the evocation of feeling.[42]

Mid-century witnessed a deepening concern for the psychological bases of taste, and an increased attention to "the psychological principles operative in critical judgments within the context of one or another of the various contemporary sciences of human nature."[43] Curiously, the theme of immediacy did not wane, nor did it lose any of the importance it had held for earlier theorists. It re-emerged as an operative constituent of the sublime and the school of taste, and its

40. *Ibid.,* p. 90.

41. *Ibid.,* p. 91 n.

42. J.T. Boulton, "Introduction," *A Philosophical Enquiry...,* p. cxxiv.

43. R.S. Crane, "Neo-Classical Criticism," *Dictionary of World Literature,* ed. J.T. Shipley (New York, 1953), p. 124.

continued strength must serve to indicate that the ontological assumptions of eighteenth-century criticism were never entirely quiescent. Harris's recharged mimesis, an amalgam of sensationalism and neoclassic postulates, cuts through the theme of immediacy and seeks to vitiate it as an important criterion of value. He fails, however, to develop any significant following because he can in no way account for intensity without immediacy, and is forced to regard poetry as essentially descriptive. Burke, of course, will hold that poetry cannot properly be descriptive and that its effectiveness rests on the intensity of the poet's conception. Furthermore, Harris's criticism does not take the affective function of art into account and so fails to keep pace with the developing values of pragmatic theory.

Most importantly, eighteenth-century criticism consistently rejected the view that art has a limited, socially instrumental function. The criticism of the period is more and more marked by an interest in the dynamics of the interactive relation between perceiver and thing perceived, and the mechanisms by which stimuli are registered, associated, and transformed in the mind. Immediacy fit into the critical patterns that sprang from these interests, and survived the decline of the older order of values with which it was associated: pictorialism – clear and distinct ideas – mimesis. The progress of this theme is in the history of mid-century criticism.

Chapter Three

Mid-Century: Impressions Immediate and Successive

What judgment should we make of the years
1719-1744? Overall, there is a certain indeterminateness of
attitude and much — too much — caution. There are no great
critics here and no sudden and remarkable achievements in the
manner of Addison's *Pleasures of the Imagination* papers. We
can, however, distinguish three specific transitional characteristics. Mimetic orientation is in transition to pragmatic orientation. The chief assumption that will now guide the direction of
criticism is that the distinctive characteristic of art resides in the
emotional effects engendered in the reader, hearer, or beholder.
Such effects are explicable in terms of certain mental processes
set in motion by the interactive relation between spectator and
work of art. Thus, the aesthetic experience provides a key to
the nature of mind; the former, if it is to be understood, must
be studied in relation to the mental processes subsumed under
the principles of associationism. Criticism now submits the
question of art's affectivity to the judgments of psychology.
Hume will soon expressly verify this shift in critical emphasis by
showing that reason cannot confidently be called the dominant
faculty of mind, but is, rather, dependent for its conclusions upon
the cooperation of other faculties.

Addison had early focused attention on the associational
activity of mind by which aesthetic delight is enhanced, and had
suggested that novelty and surprise be utilized to call forth this
activity.[1] Even before Addison, Bouhours in France had
opposed Boileau's "correctness" with the spirit of *delicatesse* or

1. Bate, *From Classic to Romantic,* p. 99.

inexactness which, in Cassirer's words, finds expression in "lightness and flexibility of thought, in the ability to grasp the finest shades and the quickest transitions of meaning."[2]

These views point to the essential character of early eighteenth century subjectivism: that the work of art is valued in proportion as it activates the imagination and excites intense emotional states. This of course profoundly affected the older and simplistic conception of art's moral instrumentality. The shift is from the view that art instructs by correcting and regulating the eccentricities of human behavior to the view that art stimulates the mind and prepares it to explore the associational relation between or among ideas, and so further creates new experience from these relations.

In effect, subjectivism, as it develops through the century, is a recognition of the vast and latent powers of the mind. Early eighteenth-century aesthetics had always maintained a severely suspicious attitude toward highly individuated experience, ridiculing it as aberrant, fanciful, or enthusiastic. So long as the *consensus gentium* was safe from attack, the neoclassical position was tenable. But the record of the first fifty years of the century reveals a series of continual adjustments of this neoclassical tenet. Consider the situation we find in religion. The Protestant Reformation had resulted in the proliferation of religious sects, each one making the claim of absolute validity. Historical Christianity was faced with a crises in which, oddly and ironically, its own energies seemed to threaten it. To escape the crisis, it attempted to formulate another version of the *consensus gentium* by abandoning any hope for general agreement on the particularities of religious dogma and shifting attention to the nature of religious

2. Cassirer, *The Philosophy of the Enlightenment,* p. 300. "An aesthetically valuable thought almost always makes use of this art in arriving at its goal, which is to startle the mind, and so imbue it with a new impulse and new energy" (p. 301).

certainty. "In founding its concept of natural religion, deism proceeds from the presupposition that there is a human nature that is everywhere the same, and which is endowed with a certain fundamental knowledge of a theoretical as well as of a practical sort on which it can absolutely rely."[3]

It is this notion that Hume assails and destroys through his examination of human nature. Contrary to the position maintained by Addison and Shaftesbury, Hume argues that human nature is not inevitably directed to an idea or sense of order immanent in the universe, but is instead a compendium of confused instincts. If we wish truly to understand religion for what it is, then we must focus our concern on those psychological forces and drives that have created it and determined its history.

This situation is analogous to the one in aesthetics. Criticism at mid-century begins to study those particular characteristics of aesthetic form in relation to their effect upon the mind and to value them accordingly. Hence, the increased attention to obscurity, intricacy, irregularity, and the concomitant decline of interest in the purely generic aspects of art and literature. Such factors as these ultimately result in the higher valuation which is given to music over painting (because the former is more "suggestive") and the recognition of the lyric as the poetic norm (because of its greater facility for compacting intensity). The implications of this line of development lead to early nineteenth-century art, which assumed as a primary function the recording of intense states of feeling and the symbolic projection of these out upon empirical phenomena: "High mountains are a feeling," said Childe Harold. This is of course to go much beyond anything stated or implied in the years 1719-1744, but even these early years evidence a still latent tendency to regard art as a short cut for the evocation of intense emotions.

3. *Ibid.*, p. 178.

The second characteristic of the criticism of this period is the growing dissatisfaction with pictorial values. Pictorialism was associated with clear and distinct ideas, and even Hartley, in 1749, can refer to the greater vividness with which painting can communicate its ideas as a principal reason for its great advantage over the other arts. Hartley, exactly like Locke before him, holds that "the ideas of sight are the most vivid of all our ideas, and those which are chiefly laid up in the memory as keys and repositories to the rest. . . ."[4] This idea, when Hartley comes to pronounce it, is already debilitated, although Kames will repeat it some thirteen years later.

A vigorous attack upon it is made by John Gilbert Cooper, who is remembered today, if at all, as an enthusiastic proponent of "taste" criticism. Cooper published his *Letters Concerning Taste* in 1755, and two years later it had gone through three editions. This would indicate that he enjoyed some substantial vogue at the time, though current opinion has it that he exerted no important influence on subsequent criticism. In Letter VII, Cooper compares poetry and painting and remarks on the adventitious aid poetry receives from metaphor. Taking as his text the line from *The Merchant of Venice*: "How sweet the Moonlight Sleeps upon that Bank! " he states:

> That verb, taken from animal life, and transfer'd by the irresistible magic of poetry, to the before lifeless objects of the Creation, animates the whole scene, and conveys an instantaneous idea to the imagination what a solemn stillness is requir'd when the *peerless Queen* of Night is, in the full splendor of her majesty, thus lull'd to repose.[5]

The metaphor speaks directly and "instantaneously" to the

4. *Observations on Man*, I, 427.
5. *Letters Concerning Taste*

imagination; painting cannot appeal with equal directness since it must first pass through the sight and be transferred to the imagination. The appeal to the imagination resides in the associational power of metaphor: the mind is delighted to perceive that the verb performs its habitual function in a foreign context. Its customary and familiar association with animal life is precisely what is transferred to warm, enrich, and "explain" phenomena which might otherwise remain remote. On the other hand, the extravagantly metaphorical conceits, which the age inveighed against from Addison to Johnson, are said to be "forced"; that is, they exceed the limits of justifiable transference. They become puns and so seemed to the eighteenth-century critics to ridicule the context of emotions in which they have their existence.

This whole reaction to metaphysical wit is not merely arbitrary or capricious. Such "mixt wit" was not usable in the sense that it did not raise ideas most apt to affect the imagination. Metaphor was not expected to be a product of a highly individuated associational complex simply because this abrogated the significance which the particular might come to assume for other minds. In short, "mixt wit" seemed the fruit of a dangerously private fancy which threatened certain key assumptions the age maintained – or tried to maintain – about the collective mind. The attitude toward metaphor is only a small part of the struggle carried on in eighteenth-century aesthetics about the relation between general and particular, objective and subjective, the universal and the local.

Where pictorialism primarily emphasizes the visual, metaphor tends to call attention to the interplay of sensory phenomena, and Cooper praises Shakespeare's metaphor for its auditory as well as its visual suggestiveness. British associationism sanctioned inquiry into the relation between all the senses and the doctrine of vibrations, and so opened the way for an understanding of the totality of response involved in the aesthetic experience. (Witness for example Hartley's discussion of the senses in chapter 2 of his *Observations.*) By mid-century English criticism had come to realize that its particular business was to understand the nature of emotional response,[6] and that the simple reliance upon pictorial values was no longer adequate.

The third characteristic of the transitional period 1719-1744 concerns the problem of immediacy. Most critics of these years agree that the highest specific function of the work of art is the immediate communication of emotion. The two chief products of the psychological approach — taste and associationism — are both, at least in their inception, attempts to justify and explain immediate affectivity and to provide a faculty structure for man's moral and intellectual nature. For British aesthetics, Shaftesbury is the seminal figure of taste criticism, and it is usually closely identified with his doctrine of internal sense. Addison, however, in *Spectator* 409 had defined it as "the Faculty of the Soul, which discerns the beauties of an Author with Pleasure, and the Imperfections with Dislike." Both Shaftesbury and Addison seem to regard it as partaking somewhat of the nature of reason, but not wholly or exclusively rational in its entirety. Leonard Welsted in 1724 reflects the condition in which they had left the term in his definition of taste as "a Faculty of Judging . . . that . . . cannot be reduc'd to a formal Science, or taught by any set Precepts," but one which a man "must be born with."[7]

Hereafter, taste split into two essential meanings. It was allied with immediate and sensuous pleasure, and with thoughtful and reflective inquiry. For Cooper, for example, the effect of taste is recognizable as "that instantaneous Glow of Pleasure which thrills thro' our whole Frame, and seizes upon the Applause of the Heart, before the intellectual Power Reason, can descend from the throne of the mind to ratify it's

6. McKenzie, *Critical Responsiveness,* p. 117.
7. "Dissertation Concerning the State of Poetry," in Durham, p. 368.

61

Approbation."[8] Though taste is composed of the refined faculties of perception, the gross organs of sense, and the intermediate powers of the imagination, these components are, as it were, blended in the faculty of taste so as to lose their specific characteristics and afford immediate pleasure.

Even Hume is not certain of the exact character of taste, but believes that reason "if not an essential part of taste, is at least requisite to the operation of this latter faculty."[9] Hume's position on the subject is largely defined by his reaction against the anarchy of subjectivism, which fosters the notion that all sentiment is right because sentiment has a reference to nothing beyond itself and is always real. Therefore, his dictum: "The general principles of taste are uniform in human nature."

Burke begins where Hume leaves off, asserting that taste must have fixed principles and that the "standard both of reason and Taste is the same in all human creatures."[10] Though taste in its principles is uniform, the degree to which these principles prevail in different individuals is various. He makes scornful reference to those who hold that taste is "a separate faculty of the mind, and distinct from the judgment and imagination; a species of instinct by which we are struck naturally, and at the first glance, without any previous reasoning with the excellencies, or the defects of a composition."[11] As taste is closely allied with the understanding, wherever the best taste operates there will we find the understanding also at work, "and its operation is in reality far from being always sudden, or when it is sudden, it is often far from being right."[12]

8. *Letters Concerning Taste,* ed. Ralph Cohen, The Augustan Reprint Society, XXX (Los Angeles, 1951), 2-3.
9. "Of the Standard of Taste," *Essays Moral, Political, and Literary,* ed. T.H. Green and T.H. Grose (London, 1898), I, 277.
10. "Introduction on Taste," *A Philosophical Enquiry,* ed. Boulton, p. 11.
11. *Ibid.,* p. 26.
12. *Ibid.*

Burke's attempt to ally judgment with taste and to make of the latter a cognitive, intellectual activity, essentially objective, runs counter to the general tendency of the age and is summed up in Kant's verdict that "The judgment of taste is therefore not a judgment of cognition, and is consequently not logical but aesthetical, by which we understand that whose determining ground can be no other than subjective."[13] This does not mean that the age was ready to give way to relativism or to surrender a hope of universal standards. The very fact of psychological criticism after mid-century is evidence enough that this was not so. We must understand the British school of taste as having its roots in a nostalgia for the experience of immediate conviction and the exaltation that attends such an experience.

Ultimately, the school of taste was a great factor in facilitating the full development of the sublime which came to assume the central position in eighteenth-century aesthetics. The sublime is the last and greatest attempt by the age to develop an aesthetic of transcendence, to remove or extend the boundaries of the finite. Basically, it predicated transcendence on the effects of the vast and obscure which challenge the individual to perceive his own isolated self before the eternal and awesome phenomena of nature. It is arguable that in a very real way the sublime offered to the eighteenth century the equivalent of a tragic theater. The point that I wish to stress, however, is that taste was an attempt to come to terms with the sudden, involuntary, and overwhelming emotions arising from the experience of the work of art, unjustified by deductive reasoning and unexplained by the theory of sense impressions.

Closely related to taste criticism — and sometimes allied with it — is associationism. Again it is Addison from whom we can take our starting point and in so doing recognize his

13. Cf. B. C. Heyl, "Taste," *Dictionary of World Literature,* pp. 412-414.

extraordinary seminal influence on British aesthetics.[14] In
Spectator 417, he explains that

> any single Circumstance of what we have formerly seen
> often raises up a whole Scene of Imagery, and awakens
> numberless Ideas that before slept in the Imagination;
> such a particular Smell or Colour is able to fill the Mind,
> on a sudden, with the Picture of the Fields or Gardens
> where we first met with it, and to bring up into View all
> the Variety of Images that once attended it.[15]

W.J. Bate develops the idea that for Addison, "since imaginative
activity in the comparison of ideas is a fundamental exertion of
taste, the use of 'novelty' and 'surprise,' which help to call forth
this activity . . . [are] valid aesthetic means."[16] Consequently,

14. Cf. Martin Kallich, "The Association of Ideas and Critical Theory:
Hobbes, Locke, and Addison," *ELH*, XII (1945), 290-315. Kallich states
that "In Addison the two significant uses of association throughout the
course of eighteenth-century criticism can already be perceived. First,
Addison resorts to association as the explanation of improper connections
between ideas and of diversity in taste; secondly, he believes that the
succession of associated ideas in the memory accounts for the *increased*
pleasures of imagination . . ." (313). Kallich's discussion relates Addison's
use of association to Locke and Hobbes, and attributes to Hobbes a
paramount role in the development of British associationist doctrine.

15. Bate, *From Classic to Romantic*, suggests that Locke had admitted
"the individual activity of the mind in receiving and combining 'primary'
ideas and in virtually creating ideas which are 'secondary' . . ." Addison,
following the principle set forth by Locke, was "led to sanction, as one of
the tests of a work of art, its ability to 'please' simply by evoking this
activity" (p. 98).

16. *Ibid.*, p. 99. The "extorting of a subjective activity in comparing
and combining ideas became not merely a conscious aim but one of the
fundamental purposes for the very existence of art" (p. 100). British
associationism "sanctioned . . . the hope for a spontaneous immediacy in

when Addison comes to discuss the "fairy way" of writing, he supports it because it is a source of vivid impressions on the imagination.

From this it followed that the mechanism of association became of central interest to the critics and psychologists of mid-century. John Baillie, for example, bases his discussion of the pleasures inherent in metaphor on the twin premises that associational activity communicates delight (a metaphor is the product of such activity), and that metaphor is itself a stimulus to associational activity.[17]

The validity of the associational relationship was generally admitted, and Hume willingly conceded that "even in our wildest and most wandering reveries . . . we shall find, if we reflect, that the imagination ran not altogether at adventures, but that there was still a connection upheld among the different ideas, which succeeded each other."[18] To determine the laws

imaginative conception, and at the same time it attempted to prove the possibility of a more or less comprehensive understanding of the particular, both in its individual 'coalesced' entirety [in which the particular is the sum of its attributes], and in the significance which it assumes for the human mind by its relationships with other objects" (p. 128).

17. *An Essay on the Sublime* (1747), ed. with introd. by Samuel H. Monk, The Augustan Reprint Society, XLIII (Los Angeles, 1953), sect. v.

18. *An Inquiry Concerning Human Understanding,* sect. iii. "According to Hume . . . objects are not necessarily connected, but the ideas are connected in our mind by association. The association is the result of repetition, of custom or habit. Two ideas have gone together so often that when one appears, it suggests the other. We have here not logical but psychological necessity, and this psychological necessity depends on experience." Frank Thilly, *A History of Philosophy,* rev. Ledger Wood (New York, 1951), p. 373. Hume here might well be considered in relation to Locke. As Kallich points out, "All his [Locke's] examples illustrate how association mars the quality of our ideas and makes them unfit for the determination of knowledge" (304). "Locke prefers to expatiate upon the irrational, unnatural trains of ideas . . ." (304-305).

governing association, Hume offers the three principles of "resemblance," "contiguity in time and place," and "cause and effect."

Hartley goes beyond Hume, and his idea of synchronous or simultaneous association is more important for literary theory, particularly in relation to immediacy. Hartley suggests a way in which we can understand the immediate reactions we have to a work of art: "some of the complex vibrations attending upon complex ideas may be as vivid as any of the sensory vibrations that come from the direct action of objects. This vividness is the result of many vibrations . . . that alter and exalt one another to such an extent that the vibrations are as vivid as if caused by reality."[19] In synchronous associations, "any part of an association will tend to call up all other parts."[20] In effect, Hartley's theory of synchronous association is a physiological explanation of Addison's observation cited previously.

Critics turned now to establishing and justifying the structure of aesthetic categories (the beautiful, the sublime, and the picturesque) on the basis of the apparatus and structure of the mind. As this happened, the theory of genres, so germane to neoclassicism, gave way to aesthetic formulae based on empirically examined phenomena. The aesthetic object and its various characteristics were studied and evaluated in terms of their affective nature. At this point, we can best study the situation in particular works of criticism, which will allow us also to gauge mid-century attitudes toward the criterion of immediate effect.

Hogarth's *Analysis of Beauty* appeared on December 1, 1753. It was not to have very much influence on subsequent criticism, although Burke is said to have been impressed by it and to have taken up some of Hogarth's ideas in his *Enquiry* of

19. McKenzie, p. 120.
20. *Ibid.*, p. 119.

1757. Reynolds, in several *Idler* papers, specifically inveighs against it and ridicules the flowing line and pyramidal figure. He especially objects to the attempt to derive standards from empirical principles and observes that "if . . . [the connoisseur] pretends to defend the preference he gives to one or the other [*i.e.*, a swan or a dove] by endeavouring to prove that this more beautiful form proceeds from a particular gradation of magnitude, undulation of a curve, or direction of a line, or whatever other conceit of his imagination he shall fix on, as a criterion of form, he will be continually contradicting himself, and find at last that the great Mother of Nature will not be subjected to such narrow rules."[21] He attacks the notion that novelty can be one of the causes of beauty and asserts that "the works of Nature, if we compare one species with another, are all equally beautiful, and that preference is given from custom or some association of ideas; and that, in creatures of the same species, beauty is the medium or centre of all its various forms."[22]

Hogarth's "Introduction" reveals his intention to reexamine the principles by which we call some bodies beautiful and others ugly. His methodology is to distinguish between the *utile* and the *dulce*, and to assign to each a certain set of characteristics. For example, regularity, uniformity, and symmetry "please only as they serve to give the idea of fitness."[23] The *dulce* is best served by variety and intricacy. In turn, intricacy of form is defined as "that peculiarity in the lines, which compose it, that *leads the eye a wanton kind of chace*, and from the pleasure that gives the mind, intitles it to the name of beautiful. . . ."[24] Hogarth intends us to understand

21. Reynolds, *The Literary Works (London, 1819), I, 239.*

22. *Ibid.*, 242.

23. *The Analysis of Beauty*, ed. with introd. by Joseph Burke (Oxford, 1955), p. 38.

24. *Ibid.*, p. 42.

that his aesthetic principles are derived empirically and so accord with the natural dispositions of the mind: "Every arising difficulty, that for a while attends and interrupts the pursuit, gives a sort of spring to the mind, enhances the pleasure, and makes what would else be toil and labour, become sport and recreation."[25]

Though he does not mention Addison by name, it would appear that the *Analysis* is written with Addison's formulae for the beautiful in mind. Where Addison had found color, symmetry, and proportion to be the specific characteristics of the beautiful, Hogarth speaks flatly against these criteria in recommending intricacy and variety. Where Addison praises greatness of manner — which is antithetical to a multitude of small ornaments or intermingled particulars — Hogarth urges in the interest of variety "the noble projecting quantity of a certain number of them [*i.e.*, small ornaments], which presents bold and distinct parts at a distance. . . ."[26]

The difference between them essentially is that in opposition to Addison's preference for Renaissance symmetry and axial design — in which we can apprehend form immediately — Hogarth proposes the baroque beauty of a "composed intricacy of form," which requires that the beauty of form be gradually discovered. Thus, for example, in Chapter 10 ("Of Compositions with the Serpentine-Line"), he examines the lines of beauty and grace, using as his illustration the figure of a cornucopia. The eye discovers the complexity of form and "is peculiarly entertained and relieved in the pursuit of these serpentine-lines, as in their twistings their concavities and convexities are alternately offer'd to the view."[27] Whoever would contravene these principles is advised to recognize the prevalence of the serpentine line in nature and in the human

25. *Ibid.*, pp. 41 -42.
26. *Ibid.*, p. 63.
27. *Ibid.*, p. 70.

frame and so come to a true understanding of "taste." In place
of a center of interest, Hogarth proposes many different centers
and an ideal of beauty that is fluid and mobile.

The *Analysis* enjoyed no vogue in England (although
some small amount of reputation in Europe) and had slight
influence upon contemporary theorists.[28] One reason is that
Hogarth's aesthetics ran counter to the doctrine of general
nature and ideal form. A second is that his *Analysis* offered
only limited attention to immediate and profound emotions.[29]
In fact he almost displaces these as a characteristic of the
aesthetic experience, substituting for them a much slighter and
frivolous one: pleasure, resulting from the eye being led a
"wanton kind of chace."

Burke seems to be replying to the *Analysis* when he cites
the "inordinate thirst for variety, which, whenever it prevails, is
sure to leave very little true taste," and mentions the triangular
form only to condemn it as "the poorest in its effect of almost
any figure, that can be presented to the eye."[30] Others before
Burke had realized that there was a whole range of affective
phenomena that could not be classified with the usual
characteristics of the beautiful and that sharp categorial
distinctions must be made among the orders of various
phenomena.[31] With Burke, however, a conception of aesthetic
form, in which the imperfect and obscure take over from the

28. "Lady Luxborough, Shenstone's correspondent . . . [went] so far as
to regret that, since her marriage, she no longer had an S in her name."
Peter Quennell, *Hogarth's Progress* (New York, 1955), p. 234.

29. See, however, Hogarth, chap. 6. "Huge shapeless rocks have a
pleasing kind of horror in them, and the wide ocean awes us with its vast
contents" (p. 46).

30. Burke, *A Philosophical Enquiry*, p. 76.

31. Cf. Marjorie Hope Nicolson's discussion of "The Aesthetics of the
Infinite," and John Dennis, maker of "the first important distinction in
English literary criticism between the Sublime and the Beautiful."
Mountain Gloom and Mountain Glory, p. 279.

regular and uniform, moves now to the center of critical thought. The beautiful is left as the antithesis to the sublime; in one view merely "a weak and sentimentalized conception,"[32] in another a phenomenon limited solely to "teaching the proper forms of social intercourse and . . . refining morals . . . ."[33]

As Samuel Monk points out, the great value of the sublime is that it "came as a justifiable category into which could be grouped the stronger emotions and more irrational elements of art."[34] Chiefly, it incorporated into itself that immediacy of response that the age, for already quite some time, had been insisting upon as the paramount effect of the work of art. The sublime provided an aesthetic theory into which immediacy fit as an integral part, a part that could not be dissociated because it was one of the recognizable signs of the true sublime.[35]

It is incontestably true that by the time of Burke's *Enquiry,* immediacy was conclusively assimilated into the sublime and was one of the unmistakable conditions of it.[36] Principally, Burke develops his idea of the sublime through a

32. *A Philosophical Enquiry,* ed. with introd. by J.T. Boulton, p. lxxv.
33. Cassirer, p. 330.
34. *The Sublime,* p. 85.
35. See Martin Kallich, "The Argument Against the Association of Ideas in Eighteenth-Century Aesthetics," *MLQ,* XV (1954), 125 -136. "In order to understand Burke, it must continually be borne in mind that in his critical system he is largely concerned with the origin of aesthetic ideas and emotions, for he contends that the origin can be found only in 'nature,' by which he means the immediate and spontaneous emotional experience. In his terminology, the spontaneous reaction of the emotions represents the way that is approved by 'nature' " (126).
36. This opinion is not at all incompatible with Boulton's statement that' "Burke's theory of Beauty found no agreement among his contemporaries and no fundamental acceptance among his successors. The same is true of his theory of the sublime" (p. lxxxviii). Boulton's remarks are intended to apply to the "terrible" sublime.

long discussion of obscurity, in the course of which he has occasion to examine the separate claims of poetry and painting to strike more forcefully upon the mind. He begins by examining the relation between clarity and obscurity in terms of the special powers of the sister arts, noting that a drawing of a palace, temple, or landscape affects the beholder only as it would have affected him in its actuality. "On the other hand, the most lively and spirited verbal description . . . raises a very obscure and imperfect *idea* of such objects," and thus "a stronger *emotion* [is evoked] by the description than . . . by the best painting."[37]

He raises only to reject the opinion of du Bos, who gave precedence to painting as an instrument for moving the passions, and develops the novel position that it "is our ignorance of things that causes all our admiration, and chiefly excites our passions. . . . The mind is hurried out of itself, by a croud of great and confused images; which affect because they are crouded and confused. For separate them, and you lose much of the greatness, and join them, and you infallibly lose the clearness. The images raised by poetry are always of this obscure kind. . . ."[38] Obscurity and the idea of infinity are conjoined in the argument that what is clear and determinate is limited and bounded, and that consequently a "clear idea is . . . another name for a little idea."[39]

Where in general the effects of poetry are not even to be attributed to its images, painting "can only affect . . . by the images it presents. . . ."[40] Further, almost entirely dissociating the effects of poetry from imagism, Burke claims that poetry moves the passions by "conveying the *affections* of the mind from one to another,"[41] and succeeds largely through sympathy.

37. Burke, *A Philosophical Enquiry*, p. 60.
38. *Ibid.*, p. 62.
39. *Ibid.*, p. 63.
40. *Ibid.*, p. 62.
41. *Ibid.*, p. 60.

As poetry is not an imitative art, so it cannot be descriptive; it must impress its effects upon the mind through the sheer intensity of context, suggestiveness, and "the combination of elements of which we have no sensory experience. . . ."[42]

Painting, however, is only an imitative art and affects "by the laws of that connexion, which Providence has established between certain motions and configurations of bodies, and certain consequent feelings in our minds."[43] This statement accurately reflects the continuity of psychological associationism stemming from Addison's literary theory. Burke, however, does not use associationism as an ontological "proof," and is less interested than Addison in final causes. Finally, Burke suggests that visual signs must necessarily represent things as they are; words convey things as they are felt. Hence the possible affective range of poetry is many times more great than that of painting.

The *Enquiry* outlined the general terms of the relation between the sister arts that was to prevail for the remainder of the century. We find frequent echoes of Burke's commentary in the writings of later critics, and Sir William Jones, for example, in 1772, is still working well within the Burkean framework. He offers an opinion on the sister arts that is merely a modification of Burke's: "the finest parts of poetry, music, and painting, are expressive of the passions, and operate on our minds by sympathy; . . . the inferior parts of them are descriptive of natural objects, and affect us chiefly by substitution. . . ."[44]

Four years after the publication of the *Enquiry*, Daniel Webb published the first of two companion volumes on the sister arts. The first, *An Inquiry into the Beauties of Painting*,

42. Boulton, "Editor's Introduction," *A Philosophical Enquiry*, p. cxxiii.

43. *A Philosophical Enquiry*, p. 163.

44. On the Arts Commonly Called Imitative," in *Eighteenth-Century Critical Essays*, II, 881.

was followed the next year by his *Remarks on the Beauties of Poetry*. By most historians of criticism Webb is ignored, and Monk's brief attention to him is prefaced with the comment that he "wrote much, but said little, on the arts of painting, poetry, and music."[45] Essentially, Webb belongs to the school of taste, but his contributions in this area are by no means remarkable. Like Burke, he believes that judgment should be allied with taste, and he adds that both have the same foundation in feeling. Judgment is nothing more than feeling improved by study and so is only a different degree of the same faculty to which taste also belongs.

This pernicious tendency to posit *faculties* and then multiply the powers or senses belonging to them, was one of the besetting ills of the psychological approach. As every essayist was inclined to make up his own list of powers, along with his own definitions of them, the interests of clarity were often sacrificed to complex and bulky systems that broke down under the weight of their own absurdity. Webb's position is not atypical. Taste he treats as a degree of an undefined faculty of the mind whose development is a process "quickened by exercise, and confirmed by comparison . . . and [which] feels in an instant that truth, which the other [*i.e.,* science] developes by degrees."[46] He holds that the immediate conviction derived from the experiencing of a work of art is to be predicated on an internal sense or faculty of the mind. Where Webb gets into a predicament (and it is an historically important one) is in trying to distinguish clearly and adequately between art and science as departments of knowledge. He appears to wish to show that the "truths" of arts are more universally accessible to mankind than those of science, on the ground that all men have within them the seeds of taste, which require only cultivation to be improved to perfection.

45. *The Sublime,* p. 108.
46. *An Inquiry into the Beauties of Painting* (London, 1761), p. 12.

Painting is not only the most natural of the arts [*i.e.*, imitates by natural signs], but its superiority is verified by its being the most useful of them: "As it is evident that paint bears the natural stamp, and very image of our conceptions, so it was natural, that men should sooner hit on this method of representing their thoughts, than by letters, which have no connection with, or resemblance to the ideas they stand for."[47] This view of painting, which to Burke was a reason for its inferiority to poetry, is now four years later offered again to forward a contrary argument.

We would misunderstand Webb's historical position, however, if we believed that his opinions ran counter to the generality of educated views. Most reviewers and journalist-critics would have been considerably more in sympathy with Webb than with Burke, even though they might not have approved Webb's notion that painting was superior to all other art forms. *The Literary Magazine,* for example, reviewing Burke's *Enquiry,* notes that he "combats the opinion of the *Abbé du Bos* . . . but surely the reason he gives is not a very good one: he gives the preference to poetry on account of its obscurity. Whereas it should be on account of its greater perspicuity, its amplifications, and its being at liberty to select a greater variety of circumstances, in order to make its exhibitions more vivid and striking."[48]

The general plan of Webb's *Inquiry* is to divide painting into its four leading branches: design, coloring, the clear obscure, and composition; to point out the different beauties and ends of each of these, and in each to note the relation of the moderns to the ancients. It is not necessary to examine here Webb's treatment of every branch; rather, it is more fruitful to consider his discussion only as it bears upon the general problem of immediacy in the art of painting. For this the last

47. *Ibid.,* p. 25.
48. *Literary Magazine,* II, 185, as quoted by Boulton, p. 63n.

two categories will be sufficient. Of the clear obscure, he distinguishes four "objects," the last of which is realized "when the particular accidents of lights and shades so cooperate, as to produce, in the general, a fine effect; and that the picture sends forth such a proportion of light, as is most pleasing to the eye, and advantageous to its several objects."[49] It is this characteristic, "the accord or harmony of the Clear Obscure, that gives to painting its first and striking effect."[50] Correggio is his model for the effects of the clear obscure, a painter who "operate[s] more by seducing the eye, than satisfying the judgment," and "the splendor of his Clear Obscure overbears our censure."[51] This sounds a little like Burke, who had noted in his discussion of light that "without a strong impression nothing can be sublime." It is worth remarking parenthetically that such hints as these provide a clue to the really major experiments in light values that were being carried on in eighteenth-century painting, particularly by the great masters of the age, Reynolds and Gainsborough.[52]

In his last dialogue, No. VII, "Of Composition," Webb works closest to the subject of immediate effects, and it is here that he is at his best and most illuminating. The entire direction of the dialogue is toward distinguishing between the immediate impression of an instant, which painting can achieve as can no other art, and the strength of the rapidly reiterated impression, which depends upon consecutiveness, the particular province of music and poetry. The whole tenor of Webb's distinction is to

49. *Inquiry,* p. 118.
50. *Ibid.,* p. 119.
51. *Ibid.,* pp. 124-125.
52. Light values change the quality of the thing perceived and so alter its "reality" for the perceiver. Different intensities of light and shadow would naturally be appropriate for the different emotive intensities of the beautiful, the sublime, and the picturesque. The work of J.M.W. Turner is the grand example of experimentation in this area. The modernity of Turner's work in the early nineteenth century is astonishing.

decide a preference between the immediate effect which instantly achieves full emotional force, then sharply declines, and those cumulative effects which progressively increase in tempo to reach a pitch of emotional intensity. Webb alternately seems to incline toward the one or other and at the last is still weighing, hesitating, and considering between them. He has, however, succeeded at least in disentangling the essential problem of comparative criticism from the extraneous factors that are frequently associated with it. He poses the question: how do we make qualitative distinctions between the emotional effects communicated by poetry and painting when each art achieves intensity via a different route? It is perhaps a question that does not admit of an answer, but much of the critical energy of the eighteenth century went into an attempt to frame one.

Increasingly, the age came to accept the shorthand proposition that the function of art is passional; it raises and elevates the mind by the stratagems of emotional excitation, or works through the affective principle of sympathy. The neo-classic formula for function — to educate and to please — atrophied and passed from the center of critical precept. By mid-century the essayists were hard at work exploring the potential cognitive values of the aesthetic experience, and trying to understand what significance immediacy and intensity might come to assume for the human condition. This situation is reflected in the new view of the artist and in the works that arise to define and defend his originality. Webb, too, shares in this emergent critical problem and elaborates on "the gift of genius, and the image of truth . . . [which] does not consist wholly . . . in the ready execution of a conceived idea; but in the immediate perception of the justness of that idea; in a consummate knowledge of the human heart, its various af-fections, and the just measure of their influence on our looks and gestures. . . ."[53] The new poet or artist is expected now to

53. *Inquiry*, p. 151.

possess the gift of intuitive immediacy, and in this lies much of the secret of his creative powers. His office is higher, though parallel, to the new man of taste (whose comic counterpart is the man of feeling), whose sensitive attunement to the aesthetic object is such that he receives its "truth" with immediate conviction.

In his *Remarks on the Beauties of Poetry*, Webb neatly scores this relationship:

> A POET illustrates one object by a comparison with another; he discovers a just and beautiful relation between two ideas: this is Genius. Aspasia feels in its whole force the merit of that invention: this is Taste.[54]

Regardless of where we look in the theory and criticism of the later eighteenth century, a conception of the role of immediacy is a vital and integral part of speculations leading to British romanticism. This is not to say that any one of these essayists is a romantic; on the contrary, they are post-neoclassical theorists working out the problems that have been left to them as inheritors of a collapsed critical system. They are pre-romantic only in the sense that their debate creates an atmosphere and a theoretical ground from which romanticism can emerge.

Webb's *Remarks* employs the same dialogue form – which he apparently enjoyed using – as in the *Inquiry*, with the exception that three speakers make up the *dramatis personae* of the former, where only two are required in the latter. The first dialogue weighs the relative advantages of the couplet and blank verse and adds little that is new to the problem. The second is attentive chiefly to the poetic image, and here Webb raises a consideration analogous to what had occupied him in the *Inquiry*. That is: are poetic images more interesting when they affect us with an immediate and single impression or when they

54. *Remarks*, p. 63.

gradually enlarge, as it were, and "keep our senses in suspense"?

He finds a relation between this second kind of image and those drawings in which, "though the parts are rather *hinted* than made out, yet the ideas are compleat; they both give a delightful exercise to our minds, in continuing and enlarging the design."[55] Webb is of course calling attention to irregularity and suggestiveness, the mind in active and cooperative partnership with the work of art, and discovering through the conjunction of a succession of ideas the justness of the design: "while we enter into the views, and obey the direction of the Poet, we fancy that we co-operate with him. . . ."[56] On the other hand, the "greatness of an image is most obvious, when it strikes us by its immediate power, and with a sudden effect . . . ."[57] Generally, the speakers agree that greatness may be achieved through either immediate effect or through the gradation of a single image, and that also, to raise a third problem, "so may it equally proceed from the arrangement or succession of different ideas."[58] Webb's very Burkean account of this last cause of greatness is that where images "crowd on each other with such force and rapidity . . . our spirits are in one continued hurry of surprise."[59] Painting can approximate some of these conditions, although not all of them, for "those images which are founded on comparison [must] be entirely foreign to painting."[60]

If we examine the sum of Webb's argument, it is clear that for him the distinctive attribute of poetic genius resides in the ability to create metaphor, which is judged according to

55. *Ibid.,* p. 79.
56. *Ibid.,* p. 80.
57. *Ibid.,* p. 81.
58. *Ibid.,* p. 84.
59. *Ibid.,* p. 86.
60. *Ibid.,* p. 91.

"the degree of our surprise," arising "from a combined admiration of its justness, its novelty, and beauty."[61] To the objection of Hortensius that surprise may be the effect of wit rather than of genius, Eugenio (Webb) answers that the man of wit "works upon us by surprise merely; but the man of genius surprises by an excess of beauty."[62] The inevitable example here is Shakespeare, whose images appeal not only to the fancy; "they do not play about the surface of an object; they carry us into its essence."[63]

Clearly, in making "greatness" the final test of poetry and painting, Webb decides, so far as he does decide anything, in favor of poetry. His methodology is, in effect, to add up the ways by which greatness is available to either art and to determine the issue on a purely quantitative basis. Since both poetry and painting can appeal with equal immediacy, Webb discovers the reason for the final advantage of poetry in the greater range and power of metaphor.

So far as Webb is admitted to have any real distinction as a critic, it must depend in large part upon his instinct for several of the key critical problems of the age; his chief talent is his tenacity in repeatedly probing the value of the immediate impression and measuring it against reiterated and successive impressions. His handling of this problem, though it resulted in no notable influence upon later critics, is surely superior to the treatment given the same problem in Kames's *Elements of Criticism,* which appeared in the same year as Webb's *Remarks.* The *Elements* is a far more systematic treatise than either of Webb's works, and Kames's reputation today is considerably brighter. But his discussion of certain important problems is far less advanced than one might expect and even unhappily conservative. His theory is largely dominated by pictorial values,

61. *Ibid.,* p. 70.
62. *Ibid.,* p. 66.
63. *Ibid.,* p. 73.

and his idea of taste represents little, if any, development from Hume. In some ways, Kames seems less to be following Burke than to be reacting against him, though J.T. Boulton states that the *Elements* "was partly written and possibly wholly planned before Burke's work could have exerted any influence."[64] In any event, we find Kames citing as inadequate those ideas that are "faint," "obscure," or "incomplete," and suggesting that the "power of language to raise emotions, depends entirely on the raising . . . [of] lively and distinct images. . . ."[65]

It would seem that Kames holds that beauty is best served by the immediate effect, whereas grandeur or sublimity depends upon successive impressions.[66] He is never very clear on these subjects, and there is some reason to believe that his position is at least highly elastic, if not contradictory. Discussing beauty, he notes that "a number of impressions in succession, which cannot unite because not simultaneous, never touch the mind like one entire impression made, as it were, at one stroke."[67] This view he illustrates through the example of geometric forms, holding it to be a self-evident truth that "a square . . . is less beautiful than a circle," and this because in the former "the attention is divided among the sides and angles . . . whereas the circumference of a circle, being a single object, makes one entire impression."[68] For a like reason — simplicity

64. Boulton, ed., *A Philosophical Enquiry*, p. lxxxii.

65. *Elements of Criticism*, ed. Abraham Mills (New York, 1847), p. 53.

66. Kames distinguishes between "relative" and "intrinsic" beauty, a distinction which parallels the familiar nicety of the *utile* and *dulce*. Intrinsic beauty he calls "an object of sense merely. . . . The perception of relative beauty is accompanied with an act of understanding and reflection. . . ." The former is "discovered in a single object viewed apart without relation to any other. . . ." The latter is "founded on the relation of objects" (p. 103).

67. *Elements*, p. 104.

68. *Ibid.*, p. 105.

which accords well with immediate effect – will a square be more intrinsically beautiful than a hexagon and, presumably, a hexagon more so than an octagon.

On the other hand, grandeur or sublimity "being an extremely vivid emotion, is not really produced in perfection but by reiterated impressions. The effect of a single impression can be but momentary; and if one feels suddenly somewhat like a swelling or exaltation of mind, the emotion vanishes as soon as felt."[69] On this basis, and measuring the relative advantages of poetry and painting, Kames decides that "our passions can [not] be raised by painting, to such a height as by words: a picture is confined to a single instant of time, and cannot take in a succession of incidents: its impression is indeed the deepest that can be made instantaneously; but seldom is a passion raised to any height in an instant, or by a single impression."[70] Thus, "reading and acting have greatly the advantage, by reiterating impressions without end."[71] Yet Kames will inconsistently assert that "the grandest emotion that can be raised by a visible object, is where the object can be taken in at one view," and "seen distinctly."[72] This criterion is never reconciled with his emphasis upon successive or reiterated impressions.

The issue is further extended as Kames continues his discussion through novelty, which lies beyond beauty and greatness and is of all circumstances that most calculated to raise the emotion of wonder, "which totally occupies the mind, and for a time excludes all other objects."[73] Novelty, like beauty (which it surpasses in the evocation of emotion), instantaneously produces emotions that being both so ardent and perfect cannot be sustained very long. (Can novelty be

69. *Ibid.,* p. 122.
70. *Ibid.,* pp. 54-55.
71. *Ibid.,* p. 55.
72. *Ibid.,* p. 116.
73. *Ibid.,* p. 131.

conjoined to sublimity, and if so, how is the instantaneity of emotion occasioned by novelty to be reconciled with the successive impressions that create the conditions of the sublime?)

Though he holds that "A picture . . . like a building, ought to be so simple as to be comprehended under one view," he thereafter adds that "there is place for greater variety of ornament in a picture than in a poem."[74] Essentially, uniformity and variety should correspond "to the natural course of our perceptions," but variety only contributes to making a train of perceptions pleasant. Returning then to geometric forms, with which Kames dearly loves to illustrate his argument, he states that "Though the cone, in a single view, be more beautiful than the pyramid; yet a pyramidal steeple, because of its variety, is justly preferred. For the same reason, the oval is preferred before the circle. . . ."[75]

For all his psychological subtlety, such universal principles as these ultimately result in a critical structure that is massively inelegant, unsteady, and dogmatic. Is this the necessary result of the empiricists' search for a "common nature" upon which aesthetic principles could be securely founded? Hear Kames as he concludes his last chapter, "Standard of Taste":

> With respect to the common nature of man in particular, we have a conviction that it is invariable not less than universal. . . . We are so constituted as to conceive this

74. *Ibid.*, p. 159.
75. *Ibid.* Bate suggests that concerns of this type "anticipate an assumption of empathy in the sense that qualities are attributed to inanimate objects or to form itself which arise from an identification of sorts, but which are determined not by the nature of these phenomena but by the place and character of the qualities in human capacity and resources. It stands opposed, in its subjectivity, to that insight of the sympathetic imagination by which objective understanding of people is achieved." "The Sympathetic Imagination in Eighteenth-Century English Criticism," *ELH,* XII (1945), 163-164.

common nature to be not only invariable, but also *perfect* or *right*; and consequently that individuals *ought* to be made conformable to it.[76]

Kames's contribution to the debate over immediacy does not really serve to further the development of this subject. His review of the relation between the immediate impression and the aesthetics of beauty and sublimity is no more than a minor historical curiosity. His idea of loftiness is still largely associated with rhetorical pageantry, with periphrasis, and with the artificial aggrandizement of the object.[77] Though he speaks of the emotions of pleasure and pain, he prefers the "agreeable" emotions that do not challenge the sensibilities or strain against emotional equilibrium. He admits that the imitation of dis-agreeable subjects may, on the whole, be pleasurable, but "the pleasure is incomparably greater where the subject and the description are both of them agreeable."[78] In no way pleasura-ble are objects of horror, which "must be excepted from the foregoing theory," for "Every thing horrible . . . ought to be avoided in a description."[79] Kames has in mind the description of Sin in the second book of *Paradise Lost.*

For all his elaborate theory, Kames is rather narrow and conservative in his attitudes and critical dispositions and has none of Burke's liberating sympathy for a variety of sensory impressions. The business of poetry remains for him a presentation of ideas of sight "because, in writing or speaking, things can only be compared in ideas, and the ideas of sight are more distinct and lively than those of any other sense."[80]

If there is no consistent development, no lucid "progress"

76. *Ibid.,* p. 468.
77. Tuveson, *The Imagination as a Means of Grace,* p. 156.
78. *Elements,* p. 409.
79. *Ibid.,* p. 411.
80. *Ibid.,* p. 325.

in the simple sense of that word from Hogarth to Kames, there is nonetheless a sustained concern with the problem of immediate affectivity and aesthetic phenomena. If, with Shaftesbury, aesthetics in the early eighteenth century moved into the center of the whole intellectual structure,[81] the problem of immediacy is now quite clearly germane to the major inquiries of British aestheticians. It is a problem to be met along all the avenues of critical debate. A few years after Kames's *Elements,* we find Shenstone in his *Essays on Men and Manners* inquiring into the hierarchy of colors and questioning "whether those that affect the eye most forcibly, for instance, scarlet, may not claim the first place . . .? "

Time and again, what is impressed upon us is the pervasiveness of immediacy as an aesthetic criterion, and in this we can recognize its major role as a unifying principle for the whole of the aesthetic structure that the eighteenth century was attempting to build. Post-neoclassical criticism turned the whole of the earlier order upside down; it called attention to the nature of man's emotive structure and studied aesthetic phenomena as so many kinds of affective stimuli. It is precisely this fact that stands out distinctively above all others and that makes the distance between, say, Dryden and Burke greater far that that between Burke and Coleridge. By mid-century, the locus of reality had been transferred to man, and literary theory was at work developing an affective link between man and empirical phenomena.

As this was so, man's essential identity had shifted from the plane of the social, civil existence, to that of the psychological. He stood forth now as a being whose identity is revealed to himself within the vague depths of his emotive nature and whose well-springs of energy and response suggest the fundamentally anarchic. Yet the age did not abandon a concept of regulated collective behavior, but hopefully moved to

81. Cassirer, p. 152.

predicate the concept of uniformity on the basis of consistently similar patterns of collective response. To this end, the eighteenth-century essayist examined a whole range of affective phenomena in the interest of establishing a new and harmonious structure of relations between man and nature. In this effort, psychology was called in to explain and justify the immediate and intense emotional experiences which began to assume the condition of a quasi-religious state of mind. My point, however, is that we are now not far from that climactic activity in which man's affective nature yields a radical insight into the constituency of genius. This is of course the bridge by which the age moved from a pragmatic to an expressive orientation, and it is a crossing that will have special bearing on the functional role of immediacy.

Chapter Four

Immediacy: Genius and Imagination

By the late 1750's, critical attention began to shift from the audience, from the qualities and characteristics of response, and the processes and faculties of mind which participate in and determine response, to the artist and his nature. This change in critical orientation, from pragmatic to expressive theory, caused the two related subjects of genius and imagination to move to the center of critical controversy. It is with these subjects, and with their special relation to the theme of immediacy, that we will be concerned here. But before we can continue this study of immediacy and its relation to the epistemology of genius, we must first retrace our ground in order to gather together some of the conclusions of mid-century criticism.

Much of the work of this period had been to inquire into the relation between aesthetic forms and their emotive effect. It had been seen and generally accepted that the highest specific function of the work of art is the immediate communication of emotion. The critical bias resulted in the classification and grading of affective phenomena according to their capacity to evoke intense and immediate response. In order to understand how stimuli are registered upon the mind and how they evoke pleasure independently of the conscious action of ratiocination, eighteenth-century criticism, from Addison forward, relied generally upon the loosely defined faculty of "taste." The exact relation between reason and taste was a matter of protracted debate; some critics such as Hume and Burke argued that reason is an intrinsic and inseparable constituent of taste. By and large, however, eighteenth-century definitions of taste emphasized its spontaneous, immediate, and non-volitional character, and also its activity in the perception of resemblances and in the comparison of ideas. These latter characteristics were predicated on psychological associationism, which guided the exertions of taste according to certain general laws or principles.

Nevertheless, the tendency to emphasize the personal and peculiar in the associational complex furthered the development of subjectivism. If, according to Hume, the general principles of taste are uniform in human nature, the personal associations generated by the exertions of taste must necessarily vary, as experience varies, from one human being to another. Further, the character of the associational complex was dependent upon the nature of the stimulus. This, we will recall, was the problem with which Webb was obliquely engaged in his attempt to measure the relative intensity of the single impression against a succession of progressively graduated impressions.

In the late 1750's, when attention was shifted to the character of the artist and criticism began to concentrate upon the nature of genius, two related problems confronted the psychological associationists. The first was to explain the relation among the separate and discrete faculties of the mind — taste, judgment, memory — and the second was to synthesize these faculties under the comprehensive faculty of imagination. What seemed, however, to be a synthesis of emotive and rational faculties of the mind resulted instead in a distribution of unequal emphases. In the new concept of genius, the non-rational areas of the mind were assigned the higher function. This was inevitably so as a new kind of inventiveness took over from the careful, purposeful activity which signified the older, neoclassic meaning of the term. Hereafter, genius was associated with the capacity for intuitive immediacy.

However, the epistemology of genius offered some serious problems. Genius could not be entirely predicated on taste, since taste was essentially a receptive faculty. Yet many of the characteristics of taste were essential to the formation of a concept of genius. The solution proposed by Alexander Gerard, in the most important of the several essays occupied with the problem at this time, was to reduce taste to a secondary power derived from the imagination. In this view all the attributes of taste were necessarily attributes of the imagination, but the imagination as a primary power was active and inventive; taste as a secondary and derivative power was passive and receptive. The advantage of this proposal was that it sanctioned intuitive immediacy of conception on the premise that the immediate *reception* of affective phenomena (taste) was merely a lower function of the mind and analogous to the immediate *conception* of a master design in the mind of genius (imagination). Fancy, in this view, served the master design by reorganizing ideas into new associative patterns when the original bonds of union in the memory had been forgotten. Judgment was called in to review and supervise the associational complex and to pronounce upon the fitness, propriety, and relation of parts to whole.[1]

Expressive theory developed logically from pragmatic assumptions; the shift from audience to artist, from perceiving to creating mind, from taste to imagination, was the inevitable concomitant of the psychological approach. The growing skepticism toward the role of reason in the entirety of man's mental processes, the increasing attention to the possible cognitive value of passional impulses and intuitional perceptions, and the relation of these to the apprehension of the phenomenal world, quite naturally encouraged criticism to concentrate on the human mind in its highest manifestation.

With these statements as prologue and as the touchstones

---

1. See Martin Kallich, "The Association of Ideas and Critical Theory: Hobbes, Locke, and Addison," *ELH,* XII (1945), 290-315. In his discussion, Kallich notes that "According to Hobbes, the judgment has two functions: it checks the overly hasty activity of the fancy when it operates in the memory only in accordance with the principles of resemblance; and it also provides in the rational principle of cause and effect a path in the materials of memory for coherent and imaginative invention" (303).

of our own inquiry, we can turn directly to those essayists whose work chiefly concerns us. In 1758, Alexander Gerard submitted his *Essay on Taste* to the Edinburgh Society. It is an often repeated fact that his work won a prize. The *Essay* consequently was published in 1759 and again five years later. Ten years hence, in 1774, Gerard published what is to all intents and purposes a sequel, *An Essay on Genius.* Together the two pieces represent the best example of associationist criticism in the penultimate quarter of the century.

In the earlier essay Gerard examines taste from a multiple of perspectives, not all of which directly concern us. The most important of his purposes, however, is to inquire into the relation between taste and imagination. To Gerard, "Taste consists chiefly in the improvement of those principles, which are commonly called *the powers of imagination,* and are considered by modern philosophers as *internal* or *reflex senses,* supplying us with finer and more delicate perceptions, than any which can be properly referred to our external organs."[2] Part I of the *Essay,* which follows this definition, is an analytical inquiry into the various internal senses (novelty, sublimity, beauty, imitation, harmony, ridicule, and virtue) and need not detain us. This list of internal senses is fairly standard for the literary psychologists, and Gerard's discussion of them does not add anything to our knowledge.

In Part II, however, his attention turns to a synthesis of these internal senses, and the comprehensive and systematic plan of the *Essay* becomes apparent. He cites the opinion of du Bos (who has by this time become the familiar straw man of British criticism) that the awakening of passion is the only business of the arts, and uses this opinion as prelude to his own discussion of the influence of judgment upon taste. Here again Gerard is not breaking new ground, but his compendious and methodical approach is designed to establish judgment as an

2. *An Essay on Taste* (Philadelphia, 1804), pp. 9-10.

inherent power of taste, and so proceed synthetically to establish that "Taste is not one simple power; but an aggregate of many, which, by the resemblance of their energies, and the analogy of their subjects and causes, readily associate and are combined."[3]

So much is prelude to his real task, that of determining how far taste depends on the imagination, a task which begins with Part III. He repeats the Addisonian formula, which had found secure place in psychological criticism, that the imagination "is considered as holding a middle rank between the bodily senses, and the rational and moral faculties," and notes again that "those internal senses, from which taste is formed, are commonly referred to the *imagination*. . . ."[4] Faced with the problem of accounting for the immediate registration of affective phenomena upon the faculty of taste, Gerard, in a long footnote, argues that the powers of taste are to be reckoned senses, noting that the

> obvious phaenomena of a *sense* are these. It is a power which supplies us with such *simple* perceptions, as cannot be conveyed by any other channel to those who are destitute of that sense. It is a power which receives its perception *immediately*, as soon as its object is exhibited, previous to any reason concerning the qualities of the object, or the causes of the perceptions. It is a power which exerts itself *independent of volition*, so that . . . we cannot, by any act of the will, prevent our receiving certain sensations, nor alter them at pleasure. . . .[5]

Though taste and sensation operate according to certain

3. *Ibid.*, p. 167.
4. *Ibid.*, p. 179.
5. *Ibid.*, p. 182.

common principles, and "As far as the sentiments of taste depend on these principles, so far they arise immediately from the general laws of sensation,"[6] taste can still be further reduced to "a derivative and secondary power." Upon further examination, "We can trace it up to simpler principles, by pointing out the mental process that produces it, or enumerating the qualities, by the combination of which it is formed. These are found ... to be no other than certain exertions of imagination."[7]

To recapitulate briefly, the logic of Gerard's argument has been to identify taste as a combination of the internal senses aided by judgment, immediately receptive and so following the general principles of sensation, and further explicable as a power of the imagination. At the heart of Gerard's conception of the imagination is the mechanical fancy: "Imagination is first of all employed in presenting such ideas, as are not attended with *remembrance*. . . . But . . . fancy, by its associating power, confers upon them new ties. . . ."[8] This faculty is prevented from being wild and lawless, though it may appear to be so, by the laws of mechanistic association which, on Humean principles, bring together ideas "which *resemble* or are *contrary*, or those that are conjoined, either merely by *custom*, or by the connection of their objects in vicinity, coexistence, or causation."[9] The associational powers of the imagination operate in all men, but "In a man of genius the uniting principles are so vigorous and quick, that whenever any idea is present to the mind, they bring into view at once all others, that have the least connection with it."[10]

So far, and not much further does Gerard go, but the

6. *Ibid.*, p. 187.
7. *Ibid.*, p. 188.
8. *Ibid.*, pp. 189.
9. *Ibid.*, pp. 189.
10. *Ibid.*, pp. 195-196.

later *Essay on Genius* represents a development from this
position, and to this we will turn our attention in a moment.
Briefly, the *Essay on Genius* is predicated on the assumption
that "GENIUS is properly the faculty of *invention*. . . ."[11] In
his inquiry into the power of mind that qualifies a man for
invention, Gerard reduces the intellectual powers to four: sense,
memory, imagination, and judgment. These he examines in
terms of their possible relevance and contribution to invention,
and decides that "genius of every kind derives its immediate
origin from the imagination."[12] Following the pattern of most
eighteenth-century theory, Gerard makes no adequate
distinction between imagination and fancy, usually meaning
either when he refers to the associating power that constitutes
invention. Thus, when he speaks of the immediacy which
attends the operations of the imagination, he means no more
than that "the power of association is so great [in a man of
genius], that when any idea is present to his mind, it immediately leads him to the conception of those that are connected with it."[13]

   To define genius as invention, invention as owing to the
imagination, and imagination as the power of producing
immediately an associational complex, is to avoid problems
fundamental to the entirety of mechanistic associationism.
Mechanistic principles alone could not explain how the more
abstruse relations among ideas are perceived by genius but
unrecognized by taste. Further, if taste and genius were
governed equally by the same associational laws, how could the
greater vigor of the uniting action in a man of genius be
explained? To say, as most associationists did, that the uniting
action is more quick and active *because* that is the nature of
genius, is to reintroduce the tautology and unbroken circle of

11. *An Essay on Genius* (London, 1774), p. 8.
12. *Ibid.,* p. 36.
13. *Ibid.,* p. 43.

imagination, invention, and genius. Most associationists seem to have thought of genius as a superior organization of common powers, improvable perhaps by maturity, education, or exertion. This view did not make a clear distinction between taste and genius, and held out at least the theoretical possibility that taste could be improved into genius.

The solution which presented itself was to relegate taste to a passive and receptive role, while emphasizing the active and inventive power of genius. In this view, which anticipates Coleridgean terms, genius was considered as a compound of primary and secondary powers of the imagination. Taste, the secondary power, was in its perfection a blending of "sensibility, refinement, correctness, and *the just proportion of all its principles.*"[14] The higher power, which Gerard based on Thomas Reid's principle of intuitive immediacy, consisted in the intuitive perception of "The existence of real things, and their connexions... [which] are inferred by an immediate judgment of Nature...."[15] Both powers of the imagination were necessary to genius, but the lower power was made synonymous with cultivation or improvement, the higher power identified with intuitive immediacy. The rapidity and vigor of the associational process is explained by Gerard in terms of the Shaftesburian conception of "enthusiasm," which makes the motions of genius "become still more impetuous, till the mind is enraptured with the subject, and exalted into an extasy. In this manner the fire of genius, like the divine impulse, raises the mind above itself, and by the natural influence of imagination actuates it as if it were supernaturally inspired."[16] Poetic frenzy. Gerard's division of the powers of the imagination was not generally recognized by other associationists, and it, along

14. *Ibid.*, p. 301.
15. *Ibid.*, pp. 283 -284.
16. *Ibid.*, p. 68.

with his paradigm of organism for the inventive process,[17] are the distinctive marks of his contribution to literary psychology.

In 1767, some several years before Gerard's *Essay on Genius,* William Duff published on the same subject. Like Gerard, Duff states that the "Imagination is the quality of all others most essentially requisite to the existence of Genius,"[18] and he develops an epistemology in all respects typical of the standard associationist view:

> Imagination is that faculty whereby the mind not only reflects on its own operations, but which assembles the various ideas conveyed to the understanding by the canal of sensation, and treasured up in the repository of memory, compounding or disjoining them at pleasure; and which, by its plastic power of inventing new associations of ideas, and of combining them with infinite variety, is enabled to present a creation of its own, and to exhibit scenes and objects which never existed in nature.[19]

Unlike Gerard, Duff does not make a division in the powers of the imagination, tending instead to regard taste as a separate and unique faculty which, when combined with judgment, is the perfection of the imagination. Judgment, taste, and imagination together constitute genius.

This conventional recipe necessitated the usual drawing forth and exchange of qualities. Therefore, imagination bestowed sensibility and refinement on taste, and taste imparted justness and precision to imagination.[20] Such

17. See M.H. Abrams, *The Mirror and the Lamp,* p. 167, for a comment on this aspect of Gerard's literary theory.

18. *An Essay on Original Genius; and its Various Modes of Exertion in Philosophy and the Fine Arts, Particularly in Poetry* (London, 1767), p. 6.

19. *Ibid.,* pp. 6-7.

20. *Ibid.,* pp. 70-72.

formulae could be infinitely varied by the associationists, depending upon which qualities any single literary psychologist wished to attach to any of the separate and discrete faculties comprising genius. Though the emphasis was on simplification and synthesis, the associationists, without an organic theory of composition, reshuffled the qualities of the various faculties into new combinations.

To explain original genius in terms consistent with "the spontaneous stroke of invention totally beyond the reach of deliberate intention, method, or rule,"[21] mechanistic associationism repeatedly emphasized the rapidity and comprehensiveness of the associational process. Duff's position will do as well as any other to indicate the position held by most associationists on this subject:

> ORIGINAL GENIUS is distinguished from every other degree of this quality, by a more vivid and a more comprehensive Imagination, which enables it both to take in a greater number of objects, and to conceive them more distinctly; at the same time that it can express its ideas in the strongest colours, and represent them in the most striking light. It is likewise distinguished by the superior quickness, as well as justness and extent, of the associating faculty; so that with surprising readiness it combines at once every homogeneous and corresponding idea, in such a manner as to present a complete portrait of the object it attempts to describe.[22]

That such views proved ultimately inadequate for the task of establishing a coherent theory of original genius is not now what is important. What I wish to stress is that the theory of immediate associative power was eagerly seized upon by the

21. Abrams, p. 186.
22. *Essay on Original Genius,* p. 89.

mental mechanists to account for the activity of the mind in creation, an activity which, according to their principles, they could explain in no other way.

Before we take leave of Duff there is one other area in which he can be of importance to us. This is in his comparison of the respective powers of the poet and painter. Duff declares for the superior affective power of the poet on the now familiar basis that it is he who has greater need for immediate associative capacity: "a greater compass of Fancy is required in the Poet than in the Painter; because a greater variety of ideas must necessarily pass in succession through his mind, which he must associate, compound, and disjoin, as occasion may require."[23] It is only the poet who can catch a multitude of evanescent forms "in one instantaneous glance of thought," whereas the painter "is engrossed by that single idea . . . which he intends to express in his picture."[24] Duff's conclusions are based on the *degree* of invention necessary for genius in either art, and his bias is governed by the implicit premise that the province of the painter is deception and simple imitation, while the task of the poet is "original," and his invention modelled after nothing that has its exact counterpart in nature.

Again the emphasis is on the instantaneity with which complex materials can be integrated into a whole, and the larger affective range of the poet. Even Reynolds, while maintaining that what is done by painting "must be done at one blow," admits that poetry, "having a more extensive power than our art, exerts its influence over almost all the passions. . . ."[25]

Attitudes similar to those held by Gerard and Duff are apparent in James Usher's *Clio: or, a Discourse on Taste,* first published in 1767 and then, with "large additions," in 1769.

23. *Ibid.,* pp. 192-193n.

24. *Ibid.,* p. 193n.

25. *Discourses on Art,* ed. with introd. by Robert Wark (San Marino, 1959), disc. viii, December 10, 1778.

Like the others, Usher is interested in that grace of instantaneous perception which defines the artist, and which he celebrates in the language of Shaftesburian fervor:

> It is to meet the sublime impression undisturbed, the poet retires to the solitary walks of the country; that he seeks for vales hid from human eye, where silence seems to take up her dwelling; and loves to frequent the woods covered with darkness and shade: there he feels, with all the certainty of intuition, the presence of the universal genius, whose immediate influence tunes his voice to music, and fires the imagination to rapture.[26]

Usher has no theory of the mind in creation that separates him from the other mechanists. His treatment of taste, judgment, and imagination is, if anything, more awkward, but not atypical of the usual patterns of associationist thought. The problem that he and they faced was the common one of trying to fit together frequently recalcitrant faculties which resisted their best efforts. Thus, Usher wrestles with the subject of taste, a faculty which, though "not ... a species of judgment ... , is actually that part of judgment, whose objects are the sublime, the beautiful, and affecting. ..." Furthermore, "this kind of judgment is not the issue of reason and comparison ... but is perceived instantaneously, and obtruded upon the mind, like sweet and bitter upon the sense, from which analogy it has borrowed the name of *taste.*"[27]

Usher merely enlarges the faculty of judgment, so that it becomes a compartment capacious enough to accommodate the

---

26. *Clio: or, a Discourse on Taste* (Dublin, 1770), p. 118.

27. *Clio,* pp. 35-36. See Martin Kallich, "The Argument Against the Association of Ideas in Eighteenth-Century Aesthetics," *MLQ,* XV (1954), 125-136. Kallich discusses Usher's protest "against the exaggeration of the associational processes in taste," and states that "Like Hutcheson and

faculty of taste. Instead of making taste a derived power of the imagination as Gerard had done, or, like Duff, leaving it a simple and discrete faculty, Usher attaches it to judgment. Such differences, however, are not as important as they may at first seem, for all three essayists are in effect emphasizing and organizing similar qualities of mind.

By 1775 certain major themes which will continue to occupy the literary theorists through the last twenty five years of the century have already been well set out. A definition of the imagination has begun to take form; among the functions of this faculty is included conspicuously its capacity not merely to imitate nature, but to rival it. The affective power of the artist is competitive with the affective power of nature itself.[28] It is this theme which, in 1772, attracted the attention of Sir William Jones, whose view is somewhat given away in the title of his work, "On the Arts Commonly Called Imitative," one of two essays appended to his *Poems, Consisting Chiefly of Translations from the Asiatic Languages*. He suggests that if a poet, musician, or painter wished to give his friend or patron "a pleasure similar to that which he feels at the sight of a beautiful

Burke, he [Usher] believes that a taste for universal beauty is originally and uniformly implanted in man by nature and that it operates instantaneously" (132). To my mind, this belief should more properly be attributed to Addison, but despite this quibble it is interesting to note how remarkably intact the Addisonian formula has remained. Even critics of various orientations and not conspicuously in the Addisonian "line" were content to adopt this fundamental assumption. As a basic tenet of belief it distinguished the uniformitarian from the relativist position.

28. See Morse Peckham's development of this subject in terms of the relation among art, nature, and "the redeemed noumenal self" in *Beyond the Tragic Vision* (New York, 1962), pp. 87-99. Peckham states that the signal achievement of German theory in the late eighteenth century was the realization that "art creates from the archetypal patterns . . . the only world that can be set over against nature, and which in terms of value is nature's equal."

prospect," each artist would gain his end "not by imitating the works of nature, but by assuming her power and causing the same effect upon the imagination which her charms produce to the senses."[29]

His classification of these arts, based in large part on the Burkean notion of affecting through sympathy, determines him to rank painting as inferior to both poetry and music, since the painter "cannot paint a thought or draw the shades of sentiment."[30] Jones's essay is another attack upon mimesis and a further weakening of the hitherto close and traditional relation between poetry and painting. It is precisely the quality of emotive ambiguity that causes Jones to place music next to poetry; the greater evocativeness and presumably the greater stimulus which the less definite representation provides the mind is responsible for the displacement of painting by music. Here again there is a shift in emphasis, in the expectations aroused in the audience. We might cautiously refer to this as the incipience of a naive aesthetic of romanticism: the value attributed to the mind being made "conscious of a variety of great or pleasing images passing with rapidity in . . . [the] imagination, beyond what the scene or description . . . can of themselves excite. . . . It is then, indeed, in this powerless state of reverie, when we are carried on by our conceptions, not guiding them, that the deepest emotions of beauty or sublimity are felt."[31] Even the conservative Hugh Blair, whose attitudes are frequently derived from Addison or Burke and all in all seem a compendium of academic opinion, states that the "happy talent [of a poet] is chiefly owing to a strong imagination, which first receives a lively impression of the

29. In *Eighteenth-Century Critical Essays*, ed. Scott Elledge (Ithaca, 1961), II, 880.

30. "On the Arts Commonly Called Imitative," II, 880.

31. Archibald Alison, *Essays on the Nature and Principles of Taste* (Edinburgh, 1811), I, 58-59.

object; and then ... transmits that impression in its full force to the imagination of others."[32]

Inevitably, the associational emphasis on the imagination widened out from artist to audience, and a broadening of what constitutes permissible and legitimate response to the work took place. If there was an attempt to maintain the validity of the *consensus gentium* in the area of the theoretical, attention also began to focus "on that which in some sense immediately concerns the individual, that is, which answers his needs and inclinations."[33] Such views were tied in with the exaltation of being that attends the experience of the sublime, with the notion that art animates and intensifies the powers of mind, with the inseparable relation between aesthetics and psychology, and with the growth of the concept of the imagination into the major topic of speculation for the literary theorists.

Post mid-century criticism had built the concept of genius on the basis of imaginative activity in the comparison and association of ideas. The literary essayists had progressively enlarged the imagination and thereby inducted into it faculties which formerly were separate from it. The next step was inevitable. In 1768, the first three volumes of Abraham Tucker's *The Light of Nature Pursued* were published; three more followed after his death in 1778. Tucker remains one of those curious figures in literary history whose position will always be marginal. He was not concerned primarily with literature or aesthetics, and his direct contribution to these subjects are small in the bulk of his work. The implications of his ideas about the imagination are, however, vital to the more sophisticated views that developed subsequently. In this he is important in two ways. First, he furthered the efforts to de-compartmentalize the mind. In his view, there was "no more

32. *Lectures on Rhetoric and Belles Lettres* (London, 1785), III, 159.
33. Cassirer, p. 104.

reason to suppose one faculty for apprehending, another for judging, and another for reasoning. . . ."[34] No radical innovation was required here; simplification was already the order of the day when Tucker's work made its appearance. Secondly, as W.J. Bate points out, in this enlarged capacity the imagination takes over whatever is gained by the conscious efforts of the understanding, making the gain "essential" and "intrinsic." Whatever the understanding registers in the mind "becomes ultimately a part of the unconscious mind, and is thus capable of being used with instinctive immediacy."[35] Ideas can be said to exist in the imagination as a perpetual "readiness" or "power" of associative response.

As this is so, Tucker provides a basis for distinguishing between conscious and unconscious mind. The unconscious is a repository of "ideas" no longer available to the conscious mind upon demand, but capable of being evoked by certain stimuli. The "mind does not call up all our thoughts directly by its own immediate command, but seizes on some clue whereby it draws in all the rest."[36] This is nothing less than in outline a theory of the mind predicated upon signal and response. Applied to aesthetics, it meant that the art object functions as a signal to the imagination to set certain associative trains in motion. Applied to the act of creative invention, it meant that the composer who has "by long practice . . . taught imagination to throw up her associations and trains spontaneously . . . has no other use for thought than just to choose the tune."[37] Where Tucker's theory fit in well with the principle of subjectivity, it did not, however, establish an effective link between signal and response. The problem of why certain signals should set off an associative pattern remained to be answered. Furthermore, was

34. Cf. Bate, *From Classic to Romantic*, p. 115.
35. Bate, p. 116.
36. *The Light of Nature Pursued* (London, 1852), I, 14.
37. *Ibid.*, 131.

each mind, in response, to be left within its own isolated and private patterns of association?

When, in 1790, Archibald Alison picked up the thread of these problems, he developed the view that "by means of the Connection, or Resemblance, which subsists between the qualities of Matter, and qualities capable of producing Emotion, the perception of one immediately and very often irresistibly suggests the idea of the other. . . ."[38] As this is true, there is no single perfect form, "or species of Forms, which is fitted by the constitution of our nature immediately to excite the Emotion of Beauty, and independent of all Association. . . ."[39] If, then, we still look for the origin of beauty, we must establish it upon subjective principles. We must look, that is, to the associations we have formed between "certain sensations and certain qualities."[40]

These associations, though admittedly subjective, are not irresponsibly personal, but are founded on a community of cultural associations. Our response to the aesthetic symbol is not based on private fancy, nor are we left isolated within the subjective patterns aroused in our minds. Like others around us, we respond to the same affective symbols; that is, to the qualities to which we have observed certain forms attach themselves. For example, in a musical composition we do not respond to the sounds, but to the emotional qualities of which the sounds are symbols. The aesthetic object is thus understood as an organization of symbols, each presumably possessing different degrees of affective power. The artist "plays" on our

38. *Essays on the Nature and Principles of Taste,* I, 187.
39. *Ibid.,* 358.
40. E.L. Tuveson, *The Imagination as a Means of Grace,* p. 188. See pp. 186-198 for a discussion of Alison and the new language of symbolism. My view of Alison's contribution to literary debate in the late eighteenth century is strongly influenced by Professor Tuveson's arguments.

emotions by arranging the relations among the symbols into affective patterns. These patterns constitute the structure of the work of art; that is, its structure is an affective organization.

Not only do material qualities possess no beauty in themselves, but as symbols they derive their beauty from the expressions of mind: "the qualities of matter become significant to us of those qualities of mind which are destined to affect us with pleasing or interesting emotion."[41] Alison's symbology again introduces the Shaftesburian analogue between the artist's mind in creation and the divine mind. Art and nature draw closer together, not because the one is an imitation of the other, but because both are unique examples of the powers and qualities of mind in creation. Both God and man are artists.[42]

The principle of sympathy had been linked with the imagination by Adam Smith, and Gerard had made of it "the medium, through which the passions or dominant associations operate in an almost magnetic creation or response. . . ."[43] Alison employs the principle to explain the immediacy with which the symbol affects us, and awakens the mind to trains of fascinating and endless imagery. The material qualities are "the signs of all those AFFECTIONS . . . which we love. or with which we are formed to sympathize."[44] These affections are "the *direct* expressions of Mind; and the material qualities which signify . . . [them] produce in us immediately the peculiar emotions which, by the laws of our nature, the mental qualities are fitted to produce."[45]

41. *Essays on the Nature and Principles of Taste,* II, 417.

42. See Northrop Frye, "Towards Defining an Age of Sensibility," *ELH,* XXIII (1956), 144-152. Frye states: "For the Augustan, art is posterior to nature because nature is the art of God; for the Romantic, art is prior to nature because God is an artist. . . ."

43. Bate, p. 141.

44. Alison, II, 418-419.

45. *Ibid.,* 419.

Alison shares with Shaftesbury, and with Addison, the doctrine that where we perceive uniformity and regularity we immediately infer design and, consequently, a formative intelligence. With both he agrees also that the purpose of art is to lead us ultimately to religious sentiment, and that the contemplation of the aesthetic artifact awakens the mind to awareness of artist and divine artist.

Empirical aesthetics had tended to abandon or circumvent the implications of Shaftesbury's position, and sought beauty or sublimity in the merely phenomenal. In doing so, the empiricists overvalued vividness and intensity and sought to make the strength of the impression the final standard of aesthetic value. As Samuel Monk explains, it is to the naive aesthetics of the sublime that we can finally attribute the vogue of the gothic.[46] The effect of this impulse in aesthetics was to vitiate the harmony which, it had been agreed, should exist between the human mind and nature, and make of the work of art merely an aggregation of organized stimuli for the purpose of inducing an exercise of the associative imagination. Alison's fundamental purpose was to correct this tendency by postulating a theory of symbolism which denied to the phenomenal world any capacity to evoke emotion independently of the human qualities that matter suggestively represented. Matter is subject to mind; the former is merely the vehicle through which the properties and qualities of mind are made knowable.

Alison's theories have never been fully studied in relation to the poetry of romanticism, and his influence never entirely gauged. Professor Tuveson has recently suggested that Alison restored to the poets "a system of common symbolism . . . very different from . . . the old. The new symbols have no objective, agreed-upon significance. They arise from the inner life of impressions and moods; they must speak to the imagination

46. *The Sublime*, pp. 212-220.

alone, for in the last analysis they have nothing to do with facts and logical reasoning."[47] It is precisely this fact about the poetic imagination *vis-à-vis* the phenomenal world that the romantics frequently dramatized.[48] To do so, they developed a use of image that is particularly fluid. Professor Wimsatt has spoken of their "blurring of literal and figurative" and "imposition of image upon image" as characteristic devices of their poetry.[49] Such devices were employed by the romantic to symbolize his peculiar and special kind of relation with nature, a relation founded upon the essential condition of dynamic mutability. Wordsworth clearly indicates this purpose in his "Preface of 1815," in which he quotes from his poem "Resolution and Independence":

> As a huge stone is sometimes seen to lie
> Couched on the bald top of an eminence,
> Wonder to all who do the same espy
> By what means it could thither come, and whence,
> So that it seems a thing endued with sense,
> Like a sea-beast crawled forth, which on a shelf
> Of rock or sand reposeth, there to sun himself.
>
> Such seemed this Man; not all alive or dead
> Nor all asleep, in his extreme old age.

He remarks in a passage immediately following that the

47. *The Imagination as a Means of Grace,* p. 190.
48. See Morse Peckham's review of scholarship, "Recent Studies in Nineteenth-Century English Literature," *SEL,* III (1963), 595-611. Peckham states that in "the late 1790's both ... [Wordsworth and Coleridge] created an epistemological revolution by introducing the imagination, the separation of the structure of the perceiver from the structure of the perceived" (601).
49. W.K. Wimsatt, Jr., *The Verbal Icon: Studies in the Meaning of Poetry* (Lexington, Ky., 1954), pp. 114-115.

"stone is endowed with something of the power of life to approximate it to the sea-beast; and the sea-beast stripped of some of its vital qualities to assimilate it to the stone; which intermediate image is thus treated for the purpose of bringing the original image, that of the stone, to a nearer resemblance to the figure and condition of the aged Man; who is divested of so much of the indications of life and motion as to bring him to the point where the two objects unite and coalesce in just comparison."[50] The poet willingly submits to the ruminations of the associative imagination which arise from the inner life of impressions and moods. In this manner, Wordsworth aligns his own powers of modifying, creating, and associating with those like and correspondent powers hidden in nature. As Wimsatt observes, "the common feat of the romantic nature poets was to read meanings into the landscape. The meaning might . . . characteristically . . . [concern] the spirit or soul of things — 'the one life within us and abroad.' "[51]

In the passage from "Resolution and Independence," the stone, sea-beast, and aged Man have no objective, agreed-upon significance; they have "meaning" only in the aggregate, and only then when they are understood as objectifications or symbolic projections of evanescent moods and states of being. Both Allison and Wordsworth emphasize reverie as a precondition for the deepest emotions and grandest harmonies. With the will and the discursive intelligence quiescent, the imagination assumes an ontological function. Being is enlarged by the re-invigoration of the inner life of impressions and moods when the will is suspended and the imagination experiences the phenomenal world (nature) in its essential condition of dynamic mutability. The stone, sea-beast, and aged Man must be understood as symbols of the romantic ontology;

50. *Wordsworth's Poetical Works*, ed. E. De Selincourt (Oxford, 1947), II, 438.
51. *The Verbal Icon*, p. 110.

that is, not as objects having more or less determinate significations. Instead, Wordsworth's romantic use of symbol suggests a psychological process having its issue in a particular state or mode of being.

Alison's great contribution to English romanticism was a theory of symbolism that opened the way for a new concept of mimesis predicated on the *natura naturans* instead of the *natura naturata*. If matter is merely the outward show of mind, the artist must not imitate the appearance, but the reality which is within; or that, in Coleridge's terms, "which is active through form and figure, and discourses to us by symbols – the *Naturgeist,* or the spirit of nature. . . ."[52] The romantic tries to apprehend the spirit or the formative process in nature, to convey the idea of "the inmost principle of the possibility of any thing, as that particular thing."[53]

Shaftesbury had advocated something very like a theory of *natura naturans,* but he had developed it through a form of intuitionalism emphasizing the microcosmic-macrocosmic relation. Alison's notion of the moral purpose of art is similar to Shaftesbury's, but the route by which that purpose is served is vastly different. Shaftesbury's aesthetic depends basically upon the concept of analogues between art and nature, artist and divine artist. Thus, to Shaftesbury, the artist is *like* divinity, and art is *like* nature; the former in each case is a reflection or mirror of the latter. This likening could not escape the pitfall of correspondences: certain forms were inherently more pleasing than others because they were better suited to lead the mind to certain moral perceptions. For art, the ultimate effect of such a

52. "On Poesy or Art," *Biographia Literaria,* ed. with introd. by J. Shawcross (Oxford, 1958), II, 259.

53. Hence, in the passage from "Resolution and Independence" discussed above, the provocative archaeological metaphors are the symbol of an experience in which the temporal and contingent are rendered timeless and essential.

theory could only be stultifying. In Alison's theory, art is the
mode of self-revelation, and mind (creative mind) works in
harmony with creative nature by imitating its spirit, not its
external forms.

Romantic theory really begins with Alison. As Shawcross
points out, for Coleridge

> although on the one hand the mind in its poetic inter-
> pretation of outward forms is limited and determined by
> the nature of those forms, yet it is equally free and
> creative in respect of them, in so far as it invests them
> with a being and a life which as mere objects of the senses
> they do not possess. Moreover, the basis of this activity
> being the desire for self-expression (not of the individual
> merely, but of the universal self), the fitness of the
> external world to be the vehicle of such expression
> pointed to its participation in a common reality with the
> self which it reflected.[54]

This conception underlies Coleridge's theory of the beautiful
and leads him to distinguish it from both the agreeable and the
good. He begins with the classically acceptable definition that
beauty is harmony ("Multeity in Unity"),[55] and that "the first
species of the Agreeable can alone be a component part of the
beautiful, that namely which is naturally consonant with our
senses by the pre-established harmony between nature and the
human mind. . . ."[56] The agreeable, in its general manifesta-
tions, and the good are both to be distinguished from the
beautiful in that the two former qualities "have an interest
necessarily attached to them: both act on the WILL, and excite

54. *Biographia Literaria,* I, lvii.
55. "On the Principles of Genial Criticism," *Biographia Literaria,* II, 232.
56. *Ibid.,* 233.

a desire for the actual existence of the image or idea contemplated; while the sense of beauty rests gratified in the mere contemplation or intuition. . . ."[57]

This Kantian theory of disinterestedness is followed by the argument which makes the beautiful congruent in its nature with "the inborn and constitutive rules of the judgement and imagination. . . ."[58] The essential similitude of self and nature is intuitively perceived, and beauty is further defined as "the subjection of matter to spirit so as to be transformed into a symbol, in and through which the spirit reveals itself. . . ."[59] The symbol which most adequately represents multeity in unity, or in which "the most obstacles to a full manifestation have been perfectly overcome," is therefore the most beautiful.[60] The symbol-making faculty of the mind is of course the imagination (opposed by Coleridge to the allegory-making faculty of the understanding): "the reconciling and mediatory power, which incorporates the reason in images of the sense, and organizes, as it were, the fluxes of the sense by the permanent and self-circling energies of the reason."[61] Imagination is related to reason (the faculty of "the intuition and the immediate spiritual consciousness of God ")[62] as an interpretative power; that is, as a power which can interpret and understand the formative in nature in the light of the consciousness of reason:

> They and they only can acquire the philosophic imagination, the sacred power of self-intuition, who within themselves can interpret and understand the

57. *Ibid.*, 239.
58. *Ibid.*, 243.
59. *Ibid.*, 239.
60. *Ibid.*,
61. *Biographia Literaria*, I, lxxiii.
62. *Ibid.*

symbol, that the wings of the air-sylph are forming within the skin of the caterpillar. . . . They know and feel, that the *potential* works *in* them, even as the *actual* works on them! [63]

The imagination, thus perceiving the "complementary aspects of a single reality,"[64] is the reconciler of those oppositions which plague and restrict the divided self, and so provides for the fundamental experience which makes possible both poetry and philosophy.

If we seek the original ground, or material cause, of the imagination, we must locate it in "the IMMEDIATE, which dwells in every man, and . . . [in] the original intuition, or absolute affirmation of it, (which is likewise in every man, but does not in every man rise into consciousness). . . ." On this "all the *certainty* of our knowledge depends. . . ."[65] Indeed, Shawcross has noted that:

As the transcendental philosopher starts from the fact of consciousness, it is in consciousness itself that he must discover the original and prototype of this activity [*i.e.,* the power of reconciling opposites]. And this he finds in the act of pure self-consciousness, in which the subject becomes its own object, and subject and object are therefore identical. Now from its very nature the apprehension of this pure self-consciousness, or pure activity returning upon itself, cannot be other than immediate and intuitive.[66]

With Coleridge, then, we return to problems that had

63. *Ibid.,* 167.
64. *Ibid.,* lxii.
65. *Ibid.,* 168.
66. *Ibid.,* lxi.

occupied Shaftesbury[67] and had vexed British aesthetics
throughout the century. Shaftesbury had attempted to close
the schism between man and nature, through the medium of the
beautiful, in the contemplation of which "man turns from the
world of created things to the world of creative process, from
the universe as a receptacle of the objectively real to the
operative forces which have shaped this universe and constitute
its inner coherence."[68] Yet without a coherent epistemology,
Shaftesbury's intuitional aesthetics rested uneasily upon an
"inner sense," and subsequently devolved into mere un-
integrated faculty psychology. This fact alone explains much of
the history of literary psychology in the eighteenth century.

Shaftesbury had formulated a theory of intuitional
immediacy which, operating through the medium of the
beautiful, allows man to apprehend the pure realm of form.
Coleridge is well within this tradition of transcendental
aesthetics; but with a more securely developed epistemology,
partly derived from Schelling, he is not liable to the one-
sidedness which vitiated Shaftesbury's intuitionalism and led
ultimately to the isolation of religious sentiment within one
mental faculty. Coleridge begins with the immediate which
dwells in every man, but does not in every man rise into
consciousness. This common organ of spiritual insight he
designates as the *reason*.[69] As intuitive, the reason comprehends
the primary imagination, "the living Power and prime Agent of all
human Perception, and as a repetition in the finite mind of the
eternal act of creation in the infinite I AM."[70] It is this power that

67. It should be clear that in relating Coleridge to Shaftesbury, I am
not awarding to the latter an extraordinary prescience; rather, I am
indicating only the continuity of theoretical problems in the critical
tradition.

68. Cassirer, p. 316.

69. *Biographia Literaria,* I, lxxi.

70. *Ibid.,* 202.

all men share; on the level of aesthetic appreciation it is the sense of beauty which *"subsists in simultaneous intuition of the relation of parts, each to each, and of all to a whole: exciting an immediate and absolute complacency, without intervenence, therefore, of any interest, sensual or intellectual."*[71]

As conscious or speculative or philosophic, reason comprehends the secondary imagination, "an echo of the former [*i.e.,* primary imagination], co-existing with the conscious will, yet still as identical with the primary in the *kind* of its agency, and differing only in *degree,* and in the *mode* of its operation."[72] The secondary imagination is the power uniquely possessed by the poet; his distinguishing character is the "power of interpreting the world of experience as a manifestation of a spiritual principle."[73] Hence, the secondary imagination is the power which "dissolves, diffuses, dissipates, in order to recreate; or where this process is rendered impossible, yet still at all events it struggles to idealize and to unify."[74] Thus, the imagination enlisted under the reason, and as primary and secondary, represents Coleridge's attempt to reconcile poetry and morality, and to assert a basis for distinguishing between creative and appreciative, between genius and taste.

In this light, it seems to me, the eighteenth and early nineteenth centuries stand in true complementary relation. The one is the logical, not merely the historical, culmination of the other. By 1790 the materials for a romantic concept of the imagination were at hand; the tremendous task of pioneer speculation and protracted debate had, if nothing else, served as a testing ground for a whole complex of interrelated problems.

71. "On the Principles of Genial Criticism," *Biographia Literaria,* II, 239.
72. *Biographia Literaria,* I, 202.
73. *Ibid.,* lxxxiv.
74. *Ibid.,* 202.

What survived was what remained important, and what remained, it had been made clear, would necessarily provide the referential bases for any epistemological theory. What did remain, and most importantly, was a theory of immediacy which had survived the vicissitudes of critical orientations. As an instrument of moral consciousness, or the ladder whereby the mind ascends from art to God; as a maxim of practical criticism in the crude hands of the early pragmatists; as an essential emotive element of the sublime; as a constitutive part of the equipment of genius; and, finally, as the determining ground or material cause for a romantic concept of the imagination, a theory of immediacy had been profoundly a part of that long journey from the eighteenth to the nineteenth century.

Conclusion

This essay has been principally an attempt to reconstruct the history of a theme in eighteenth-century literary theory. A history of the sort that I have written does not change the configurations of the literary theory as we know it, but it does suggest the continuity of a unifying principle about which we may not have known. Therefore, I would hope that *immediacy* in its dual significance as a criterion of value in aesthetic judgments and as an intuitive faculty and so determining ground for the concepts of taste, genius, and imagination, will be of some use to other historians of criticism. Such meanings are of course not disharmonious, but on the contrary represent a profound attempt to align the immediately emotive (in the phenomenal world) with the intuitively immediate (in the nature of being). Where the romantic *projects* value from within out upon phenomena, the Augustan *discovers* value in the immediate responses of his affective structure. The Augustans' exploration and development of this structure was one of the last serious attempts to resist the fragmentation of self and the dislocation of a communal identity, which are among the conditions of our modern experience. The eighteenth-century emphasis upon affectivity is consistent with the repeated attention given to what is general, rather than uniquely particular, in experience. Blake, for example, proved himself a *new* man by his rejection of Reynolds's standard; and Arnold, in the spirit of liberal, humanist, egalitarian sentiments, confounded the emphasis upon order and decorum with the cold and repressive and provided a rationale for it in keeping with the nineteenth-century myth of historical necessity.

Ironically, of course, "regularity, uniformity, precision, balance," served both formal-mimetic and moral-affective criteria in the early eighteenth century. The romantic artist, however, with his greater interest in process than in product, and in mutability rather than stasis, frequently dramatized (a) the original processes whereby a poem comes into being, and (b) the impact of force acting upon form to render flux and make visible the mutable.[1] The romantic tries first to make us respond to what is within the self, what wells up from the unconscious and is projected in the archetypal symbols of cavern, stream, forest, etc. The Augustan seeks to discover the relevance of what which is outside the self to the self; that is, he thinks of the self as seeking the proper harmony with the knowable "good." He empirically examines phenomena in terms of their capacity to affect the moral consciousness; the "grand" is a real entity in nature, and certain kinds of stimuli raise the mind to an awareness of it. The process of discovering an affective relation between self and nature is not dramatized because it is inherently undramatic (*i.e.*, without conflict), whereas the kinds and qualities of affective stimuli are frequently discussed at great, even tedious length.

At one end of the century is Addison; at the other is Alison. Both are symbolists, but as Professor Tuveson has made us aware, "the Addisonian theory is an unrecognized one of symbolism."[2] Both utilize a theory of human nature in which the intuitionally immediate functions as a constituent law of being to direct our responses to and beyond certain kinds of affective phenomena. In the sustained debate over what these phenomena were or should be, the specific requirement of immediate effect served as the usual touchstone of aesthetic

1. See, for one example among many, Ruskin's moral-affective discussion, "Of Water, as Painted by Turner": "Few people, comparatively, have ever seen the effect on the sea of a powerful gale continued without intermission for three or four days and nights; and to those who have not, I believe it must be unimaginable, not from the mere force or size of the surge, but from the complete annihilation of the limit between sea and air" (*Modern Painters,* Part II, Sect. v, Chap. 3.)

2. *The Imagination as a Means of Grace,* p. 188.

value. That this was so is evident from the fact that such diverse characteristics as uniformity and irregularity, order and disorder, were argued with equal conviction before the same standard of immediacy.

Burke, we will recall, opposed the pictorial values of clear and distinct ideas with those affective criteria to which the immediate effect was intrinsic. And Webb and Kames both attempted to distinguish the sublime from the beautiful on the basis of successive or immediate impressions. The earlier comparatists of poetry and painting had frequently decided between the sister arts on a like basis, and Jonathan Richardson's dictum (that painting "pours" ideas into the mind, whereas words only "drop" them) was reiterated with enough frequency to become the crux of various critical contentions. To intuitional moralists like Shaftesbury, or associationists like Gerard, the principle of immediacy served to explain the action of the mind in creation as it could be explained in no other way. When in the early nineteenth century, Coleridge tried to formulate a theory of the imagination, he drew upon bases of thought that were native to the British tradition and upon modes of psychological inquiry that had been practiced at least a half century earlier. This history, then, has tried to set before the reader these and like determinations in theory and criticism.

L.A. Elioseff has recently suggested that "The total structure of the history of criticism as a chapter in cultural history is a universe of discourse composed of a number of critical systems. . . ."[3] The effort of this study has been to disclose the commonly relevant within (in terms of my own intentions) a century of continuous discourse. The principle of immediacy served eighteenth-century theory as a common principle for ontological, psychological, and aesthetic inquiries. It is for this reason that I prefer to think of this essay as the synthetic study of a theme – to distinguish it from mere

3. *The Cultural Milieu of Addison's Literary Criticism*, p. 17.

historical journalism and from the larger, more broadly inclusive and interpretative goals of cultural history.

Synthesis is the art of integrating the relevant; immediacy has been for us the vehicle for determining patterns of relevance, for exploring the boundaries of contiguity and contingency in the discrete schools and systems of aesthetic-literary thought. Thus, I hope that the consistently relevant theme of immediacy will offer a fresh means for revaluating the modes and intentions of eighteenth-century criticism, a revaluation which is in progress, which has been long overdue, and to which this essay modestly endeavors to contribute.

BIBLIOGRAPHY

Abrams, M. H. *The Mirror and the Lamp: Romantic Theory and the Critical Tradition.* New York, 1953

Addison, Joseph, and Richard Steele. *The Spectator,* ed. Donald Bond. Oxford; Clarendon Press, 1965.

Alison, Archibald. *Essays on the Nature and Principles of Taste.* 2 vols. Edinburgh, 1811.

Arbuckle, James. *A Collection of Letters and Essays . . . Lately Published in the Dublin Journal . . .* 2 vols. London, 1729.

Arnold, Matthew. *Essays in Criticism: Second Series.* London, 1905.

Baillie, John. *An Essay on the Sublime,* ed. with introduction by S.H. Monk. The Augustan Reprint Society, XLIII. Los Angeles, 1953.

Bate, W.J. *From Classic to Romantic: Premises of Taste in Eighteenth-Century England.* Cambridge, Mass., 1946.

———. "The Sympathetic Imagination in Eighteenth-Century English Criticism," *ELH,* XII (1945), 144-164.

Blair, Hugh. *Lectures on Rhetoric and Belles Lettres.* 3 vols. London, 1785.

Bloom, Edward A. and Lillian D. "Addison's 'Enquiry after Truth': The Moral Assumptions of his Proof for Divine Existence,"*PMLA,* LXV (1950), 198-220.

Boyd, John S., S.J. *The Function of Mimesis and its Decline.* Harvard University Press, 1968.

Brett, R.L. "The Aesthetic Sense and Taste in the Literary Criticism of the Early Eighteenth-Century," *RES,* XX (1944), 199-213.

Bullitt, J.M. "Hazlitt and the Romantic Conception of the Imagination," *PQ,* XXIV (1945), 343-361.

Burke, Edmund. *A Philosophical Enquiry into the Origins of our Ideas of the Sublime and Beautiful,* ed. J.T. Boulton. New York, 1958.

Cassirer, Ernst. *The Philosophy of the Enlightenment.* Princeton University Press, 1951.

Coleridge, S.T. *Biographia Literaria,* ed. with his *Aesthetical Essays* by J. Shawcross. 2 vols. Oxford, 1958.

Cooper, Anthony Ashley [Third Earl of Shaftesbury]. *Characteristicks of Men, Manners, Opinions, Times.* 3 vols. [London], 1732.

Cooper, John Gilbert. *Letters Concerning Taste.* London, 1755, and as edited by Ralph Cohen, The Augustan Reprint Society, XXX. Los Angeles, 1951.

Crane, R.S. "Neo-Classical Criticism," *Dictionary of World Literature,* ed. Joseph T. Shipley. New York, 1953, pp. 116 -127.

Dryden, John. *Essays,* ed. W.P. Ker. 2 vols. New York, 1961.

Du Bos, Jean Baptiste. *Critical Reflections on Poetry, Painting, and Music.* 3 vols. London, 1748.

Duff, William. *An Essay on Original Genius: and its Various Modes of Exertion in Philosophy and the Fine Arts, Particularly in Poetry.* London, 1767.

Durham, W.H.*Critical Essays of the Eighteenth Century, 1700 -1725.* London, 1915.

Elioseff, L.A. *The Cultural Milieu of Addison's Literary Criticism.* Austin, Texas, 1963.

Elledge, Scott. *Eighteenth-Century Critical Essays.* 2 vols. Ithaca, New York, 1961.

Frye, Northrop, "Towards Defining an Age of Sensibility," *ELH,* XXIII (1956), 144 -152.

Gerard, Alexander. *An Essay on Genius.* London, 1774.

–––. *An Essay on Taste.* Philadelphia, 1804.

Hagstrum, Jean H. *The Sister Arts: The Tradition of Literary Pictorialism and English Poetry from Dryden to Gray.* Chicago, 1958.

Harris, James. *Three Treatises . . . .* London, 1772.

Hartley, David. *Observations on Man.* 2 vols. London, 1791.

Heyl, B.C. "Taste," *Dictionary of World Literature,* ed. Joseph T. Shipley, New York, 1953, pp. 412 -414.

Hipple, W.J., Jr. *The Beautiful, the Sublime, and the Picturesque in Eighteenth-Century British Aesthetic Theory.* Carbondale, 1957.

Hogarth, William. *The Analysis of Beauty,* ed. with introduction by Joseph Burke. Oxford, 1955.

Home, Henry, Lord Kames. *Elements of Criticism,* ed. Abraham Mills. New York, 1842.

Hume, David. *An Inquiry Concerning Human Understanding.* New York, 1955.

–––. *Essays Moral, Political, and Literary,* ed. T.H. Green and T.H. Grose. 2 vols. London, 1898.

Jacob, Hildebrand. *Works.* London, 1735.

Johnson, Hames W. *The Formation of Neo-Classical Thought.* Princeton, 1967.

Kallich, Martin. *The Association of Ideas and Critical Theory in Eighteenth-Century England.* The Hague: Mouton, 1970.

–––. "The Argument Against the Association of Ideas in Eighteenth-

Century Aesthetics," *MLQ,* XV (1954), 125 -136.

———. "The Association of Ideas and Critical Theory: Hobbes, Locke, and Addison," *ELH,* XII (1945), 290 -315.

Lamotte, Charles. *An Essay upon Poetry and Painting.* Dublin, 1742.

Locke, John. *An Essay Concerning Human Understanding,* ed. Alexander C. Fraser. 2 vols. New York, 1959.

Lovejoy, A.O. *Essays in the History of Ideas.* Baltimore, 1948.

McKenzie, Gordon. *Critical Responsiveness: A Study of the Psychological Current in Later Eighteenth-Century Criticism.* University of California Publications in English, XX. Berkeley and Los Angeles, 1949.

Monk, S.H. *The Sublime: A Study of Critical Theories in XVIII-Century England.* New York, 1935.

Nicolson, Marjorie Hope. *Mountain Gloom and Mountain Glory: The Development of the Aesthetics of the Infinite.* Ithaca, New York, 1959.

Peckham, Morse. *Beyond the Tragic Vision: The Quest for Identity in the Nineteenth Century.* New York, 1962.

———. "Recent Studies in Nineteenth-Century English Literature," *SEL,* III (1963), 595 -611.

Quennell, Peter, *Hogarth's Progress.* New York, 1955.

Reynolds, Sir Joshua. *Discourse on Art,* ed. with introduction by Robert Wark. San Marino, 1959.

———. *The Literary Works of Sir Joshua Reynolds.* 3 vols. London, 1819.

Richardson, Jonathan. *Works.* London, 1792.

Ruskin, John. *The Complete Works,* ed. E.T. Cook and A. Wedderburn. 39 vols. London, 1903 -1912.

Spingarn, J.E. *Critical Essays of the Seventeenth Century.* 3 vols. Oxford, 1957.

Thilly, Frank. *A History of Philosophy,* rev. Ledger Wood. New York, 1952.

Thorpe, C. DeWitt. "Addison and Hutcheson on the Imagination," *ELH,* II (1935), 215 -234.

Tucker, Abraham. *The Light of Nature Pursued.* 2 vols. London, 1852.

Turnbull, George. *A Treatise on Ancient Painting.* London, 1740.

Tuveson, Ernest L. *The Imagination as a Means of Grace: Locke and the Aesthetics of Romanticism.* Berkeley and Los Angeles, 1960.

Usher, James. *Clio: or, a Discourse on Taste.* Dublin, 1770.

Webb, Daniel. *An Inquiry into the Beauties of Painting.* London, 1761.

———. *Remarks on the Beauties of Poetry.* London, 1762.

Wellek, René. *A History of Modern Criticism: 1750 -1950.* 2 vols. New Haven, 1955.

Wimsatt, William K., Jr. *The Verbal Icon: Studies in the Meaning of Poetry.* Lexington, Kentucky, 1954.

Wordsworth, William. *Poetical Works,* ed. Ernest de Selincourt and Helen Darbyshire. 5 vols. Oxford, 1941-1949.

INDEX

Synchronous association, 65; *see also* Association of Ideas
Taste, 6, 7n, 11, 31, 43, 52, 58, 60-63, 63n, 68, 72, 76, 79, 86-97,
    96n-97n, 111, 113
Thorpe, C. DeWitt, 22n, 26n
Tragedy, 27, 30, 36, 45, 48, 62
Tucker, Abraham, 99 -100
    The Light of Nature Pursued, 99 -100
Turnbull, George, 41-44
    and the moral sense, 43
    and taste, 43
    A Treatise on Ancient Painting, 41-44 •
Turner, J.M.W., 74n, 114n
Tuveson, Ernest L., 8, 8n, 13, 26, 101n, 103, 114
Uniformity, 13, 14, 15, 18, 19, 20, 21, 23, 24, 42, 61, 66, 69, 81, 84, 103,
    113, 115
Usher, James, 95 -97, 96n-97n
    Clio: or, a Discourse on Taste, 95 -97
Ut Pictura Poesis, 27, 33
Variety, 66, 67, 68, 81
Webb, Daniel, 10, 12, 71-78, 86, 115
    Inquiry into the Beauties of Painting, 71, 72 -75
    Remarks on the Beauties of Poetry, 72, 76 -78
Wellek, Rene, 11
Welsted, Leonard, 60
    and taste, 60
Wimsatt, William K., Jr., 104, 105
Wit, 39, 78
    metaphysical, 59
    "mixt," 59
Wolseley, Robert, 28
Wordsworth, William, 104 -106, 104n
    "Preface of 1815," 104
    "Resolution and Independence," 104 -105